D0936365

The LAWs of the Golf Swing

The LAWs of the GOLF SWING

Body-Type Your Swing and Master Your Game

Mike Adams,
T. J. Tomasi, and
Jim Suttie

HarperCollins*Publishers*

HarperCollins*Publishers* gratefully acknowledges Metropolitan Life Company, *Statistical Bulletin,* which granted permission to reprint its height and weight chart on pages 43–44.

All photographs by either Terry Renna or Warren Raatz.

THE LAWS OF THE GOLF SWING. Copyright © 1998 by Mike Adams, T. J. Tomasi, and Jim Suttie. All rights reserved. Printed in the United States of America. No part of this book may be used or reproduced in any manner whatsoever without written permission except in the case of brief quotations embodied in critical articles and reviews. For information address HarperCollins*Publishers*, Inc., 10 East 53rd Street, New York, New York 10022.

HarperCollins books may be purchased for educational, business, or sales promotional use. For information please write to Special Markets Department, HarperCollins*Publishers*, Inc., 10 East 53rd Street, New York, New York 10022.

Designed by Irving Perkins Associates

FIRST EDITION

Library of Congress Cataloging-in-Publication Data
Adams, Mike. 1954–
     The LAWs of the golf swing : body-type your swing and master your game / Mike Adams, Jim Suttie and T.J. Tomasi. — 1st ed.
  ISBN 0-06-270815-5
  1.   Swing (Golf) 2. Somatotypes. I. Suttie, Jim. II. Tomasi, T. J. III. Title.
  GV979.S9A284 1998   98–10674
  796.352'3—dc21   CIP

02 ❖/RRD 10 9 8 7

Contents

The authors give special thanks to Kathryn Maloney, who not only edited the text but who also helped to shape the model by sharing her knowledge about the golf swing with us; to Mike McGetrick, our friend and colleague, who gave us feedback and direction as the LAWs model grew; to Warren Raatz, for his excellent photographs and for the many behind-the-scenes labors that helped bring the LAWs to press; to Gary Perkinson, for his errorless copyediting; and, finally, to John Gardner, the Director of Golf at PGA National Resort in Palm Beach Gardens, Florida, for his support and encouragement.

How the LAWs Came About

The Search

It was 1991 when the three of us, all experienced teachers, began to consider what we knew to be a problem in golf instruction: with all the advances in technology, with the dedication of the largest professional sports organization in the world, with the multibillion-dollar interests of the business world at stake, the average handicap had hardly changed in thirty years. As teachers dedicated to making golfers better, we asked ourselves how this could be possible.

We concluded that one culprit is the *way* in which golf is often taught and written about, treating all golfers the same regardless of their physical attributes. Tall and thin, short and powerful, stiff as a board, loose as a noodle—in conventional teaching they all learn the same concepts and swing mechanics, and they're all asked to perform the same physical movements. Now, you wouldn't go to a doctor who automatically performed the same operation on every patient irrespective of his illness, or to an investment counselor who gave every client the same portfolio—but you might unknowingly go to a golf teacher who scrunches everyone into the same mold regardless of crucial individual differences.

It was through experimentation that we came to believe that golf-swing mechanics must vary with golfers' body types.

Granted, there are many variations among the golf swings of the pros. Nobody is going to confuse Lee Trevino with Fred Couples.

Ernie Els is nicknamed "The Big Easy" for his ultrasmooth swing, yet Jim Furyk's swing has been likened to a man trapped in a phone booth with a poisonous snake. So what do they all have in common, other than the fact that they all play world-class golf? The LAWs model (an acronym for leverage/arc/width swing) answers that good players have found a way to match their technique to their physique. Can you imagine trying to swing like Davis Love when you're built like Craig Stadler, or vice versa? They are both great players, and that means that when it comes to hitting a golf ball, they both satisfy the laws of physics at impact. But because of their body types—Love is tall with long levers and a thin chest, whereas Stadler is stocky with a barrel chest—they get the job done differently. The bottom line is that each uses a swing that perfectly matches his unique characteristics of body build, strength, and flexibility. The cornerstone of the LAWs model is that *golf is hard only when you ask your body to do things it can't do.*

Even the world's best golfers must adhere to the physique/technique matchup rule to maintain their winning ways. There have been many horror stories about golfers who somehow got mismatched and fell from grace.

At the top of his game, Johnny Miller inadvertently changed his body by doing heavy work on his ranch. When he returned to competition a few months later, his game was gone, and he struggled to regain his form. Even the greatest player of all time, Jack Nicklaus—ravaged by injury and decreasing flexibility—has become just another good senior player because he's unable to change his swing to harmonize with the aging process.

No-Fault Assurance

The point is, if mismatching is so ruinous to the game's best players, who spend hours on the practice tee with custom-fitted equipment, superb hand-eye coordination, and peak physical fitness, just think what it can do to the average golfer. Golf is hard not because of some intrinsic difficulty in the game or some innate lack of skill on the part of the general golfing public. It's hard because most golfers have a swing that doesn't fit them. It's a great comfort when you realize that if you're struggling with your game, it's *not your fault—you're just mismatched.*

How Did You Become Mismatched?

As we've said, a teacher at some point might have unknowingly scrunched you into a swing method that works fine for other body types but not for yours. This is akin to fitting everyone with the same shoe size because you've discovered the essence of "shoeness."

In other cases you might have chosen the wrong golfer to copy. Too often we see short, muscular fifty-year-olds trying to swing like Fred Couples and tall, thin players whose model is Ben Hogan. Or maybe you like to tinker and don't stick with anything long enough to make it permanent. Let's face it: golfers, for the most part, are a promiscuous lot—they will lie down with almost any swing theory that comes along, no matter how wacky it is. And there is no quicker way to get mismatched than by tinkering—building a golf swing with a grip from one method, a takeaway from another, and a downswing from still another, producing a Frankenstein-like amalgam of mismatched parts that neutralizes whatever talent you have for the game. And, as we shall see, your time IQ—how well you time your golf swing—also plays a major role in the matching game. When you lose control of it, you lose control of your swing.

Our research makes it clear that at least two out of three golfers are victims of a mismatch between their swing type and their body type. Once you fall victim to this mismatching, it becomes almost impossible for you to maximize your potential to play the game; using the wrong swing type, you accentuate your weaknesses and neutralize your strengths.

We believe the LAWs model is the best way to build your golf swing because it provides guidelines for matching your swing to your body build—it gives you a *personalized* swing model, adapted to your unique body type. This book shows you how to identify your body type, choose the correct swing type, and how to learn your swing model.

Where Does the Model Come From?

The LAWs of golf model comes from extensive observation of what works, coupled with a little knowledge of physics, biomechanics, and the fundamentals of a sound golf swing. Many good teachers have taught this way, even though they might not have articulated it in such detail or even realized they were doing it. Explaining the LAWs model to our colleagues, we've often found that its simplicity and thoroughness is so compelling that many say, "Why, of course that's true—I've been teaching like that for years," thus confirming the model's power to foster an awareness of what was there all along.

There is a historical sequence characteristic of all effective models. First, the new model is ignored by experts in the field. Then, as it proves itself at the grassroots level, the experts argue that it doesn't work. Finally, when it becomes clear that the model is a powerful tool, they claim to have invented it.

We're at the point now, after seven years of research, where we can tell you that the LAWs model does work. We've tested it in our golf schools and in our private lessons on players whose skill levels range from beginner to tour player. We've studied hundreds of hours of videotape of the swings of the greatest players of all time, the true masters of the game. Together the three of us have a total of more than seventy years experience in golf instruction and have given well over a hundred thousand lessons, and the culmination of that experience is the LAWs of golf model.

The power that the LAWs has to create perfect matches has already received resounding endorsements. The superstar Greg Norman has licensed the right to use the LAWs of golf in his instructional tape series. The LAWs has captured the public's imagination through the many articles that have been written, especially a March 1996 cover story in *Golf* magazine, an issue that had the phones ringing off the hooks at the magazine's headquarters. The PGA, which has a membership of more than twenty thousand golf professionals, has asked us to give presentations to its members on the LAWs, and we estimate that the LAWs of golf is already used by over thirty thousand devotees worldwide. As Robert Lohrer, editor-in-chief of *Golf Pro* magazine, wrote in 1996 about the importance of the LAWs, "Marrying body types to swing types isn't just a good idea—it's the LAWs of golf!" Even President Bill Clinton, our country's number one golfer, has taken lessons in the LAWs of golf.

1

Bursting the Bubble That All Swings Are the Same

Studies performed at the research labs of True Temper distinguish three swing profiles, each of which shows the golfer loading the club shaft differently. Loading is the bending of the club shaft in the toe-up direction relative to the address position. It begins in the transition zone from backswing to downswing and causes your club head to lag behind the shaft. Unloading occurs when the shaft loses its load, reverses its bend, and releases the club head into the toe-down position, thereby emptying its energy into the ball.

The three load profiles are measured in time from the top of the swing. The double-peak profile shows the first loading peak occurring early in the downswing, with the second load coming a few tenths of a second later. It has two bursts—two places in the downswing where the bend in the shaft noticeably changes. In the single-peak profile, load maximizes early, and then declines steadily until impact; it has one burst. The last profile, known as the "ramp-up" swing, shows steadily building pressure on the shaft until the load is released just before impact. It has no bursts.

The bowing of the shaft indicates that loading is taking place.

In the diagram the three appear superimposed on one another.

While the studies were not done with our LAWs model in mind, they correlate nicely with the LAWs model, which classifies the dou-

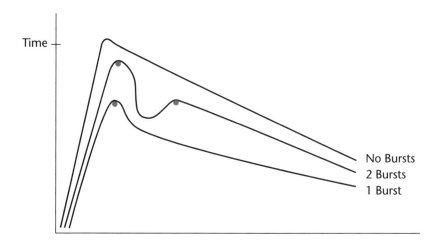

ble-peak profile, with its two bursts of loading, as the medium-tempo leverage swing, like that of David Frost and Nick Faldo. The single-peak profile, with its early, single burst of load, correlates with the fast-paced muscular-advantage swing exemplified by Nick Price and Craig Stadler. The unhurried pace of the no-burst, ramp-up swing, in which pressure builds slowly toward the climax of impact, is typical of arc players such as Phil Michelson and Fred Couples.

On Learning the LAWs Model: Two Pieces of Advice Before You Start

THE BALL AS MASTER

A major block to learning is allowing the ball to be your master and therefore making changes in your swing based on the previous shot. If ball flight is your only evaluation system, you'll spend most of your time tinkering with your swing.

Say you're working on something new, like a takeaway change. If you hit sixty balls and thirty fly well, you don't make any changes. But had you made a change after each shot that wasn't good, you would have made thirty changes in just one practice session, and no golf swing can survive that many changes. Why? Because when the ball is your master, you'll go through a cycle of constant adjustments, not only changing something wrong into something right, but also changing something right into something wrong, and so on ad infinitum, preventing you from developing a dependable golf swing.

When ball flight controls the learning process, you can't stay focused. Let's say you're working on the grip and you hit a few shots that don't go where you want them to. Now if you abandon what you were working on to get the ball to go straight, you'll never learn the grip. The way you incorporate a new grip into your blueprint is by matching the model grip perfectly and then repeating it until you learn it, regardless of where the ball goes.

Here's a good rule to follow: when you're learning a "swing piece," your evaluation system should be how well you match the model, not the flight of the ball. Once you have your blueprint in place, you can troubleshoot your swing on the basis of the ball's flight. In this case, however, ball flight is your servant, not your master. It allows you to repair your swing based on your owner's maintenance manual (the LAWs model), thereby preserving rather than destroying the blueprint.

WINDOW OF VULNERABILITY

Research from Johns Hopkins University shows that to learn a new skill, it's not enough simply to practice it; after practicing a skill, you have to allow enough time for the brain to encode the information. For about six hours after you learn a motor skill—such as the setup, takeaway, or the wrist cock—there is a *window of vulnerability* during which the new skill can be erased from your memory if you try to learn another skill on top of it. This is why students often get confused and discouraged when trying to learn golf. The problem is not the amount of information you're receiving about any one skill or task but the number of tasks presented all at once. You can absorb a lot of information about the task you're learning, but if there isn't a sufficient incubation period between tasks, your brain will forget what you learned.

This is why we've broken down the LAWs model into distinct segments, each made up of a family of related minitasks that combine to form a task unit. Once the unit is learned, there should be a spacing of at least six hours before you learn the next task unit. So to learn the setup from your first task unit, the preparation stage, match the model for your swing type, take your grip, check your ball position, flare your feet, and so on. Check your stance in a mirror (or on videotape), and keep a Polaroid picture and/or a copy of the LAWs book right there on the driving range as a reference. Take some practice swings, and then hit balls, making sure before every swing that you're matching your model. Now you can see why you should ignore the ball flight—all you should care about at this point is how well you're doing this task. Once you're done, stop and let it sink in. Or as Chuck Hogan puts it, achieve and then leave. Come back the next time, and begin with the next task, which in this case would be learning the takeaway.

So when you're learning your LAWs swing, don't let the ball be your master, and observe the window of vulnerability.

2

Research from the Trenches

In part, our research came from the lesson tee; as hands-on teachers, we have never lacked for subjects. Once we developed the concept of matching the swing to the body, we began to experiment with it to see if we could get better results — even if it meant defying some of the entrenched theory about what a swing should look like and how it should be taught. We found that when we made certain unconventional changes, the results bordered on the spectacular. This finding led us to overturn even more of the conventional wisdom of golf instruction. Our results told us we were on to something.

Barrel Man

An outstanding example was a middle-aged golfer from New York — we'll call him Barrel Man because of the size of his chest. Short and stocky, with a big chest and short, muscular arms, he had minimal flexibility but exceptional strength and was frustrated because he tended to hit the ball fat or to hit a weak slice. The discouraging results of this off-target array of shots were scores that were much too high for his athletic ability.

With his left arm bending until his hands almost touched his right ear, his swing, at the top, was much too long and out of control. Even so, his address mechanics appeared sound: the ball was played forward in his stance, opposite his left heel, his stance was square, and his grip was right out of the book.

Trying for a long, high swing, Barrel Man bends his left elbow. He's been told to keep his head down, and it causes him to hang on to his left side.

Here was an individual with an "unofficial" body build who had been given standard-issue instruction. Basically, he was a good learner who was a victim of the paradox that the LAWs model is meant to solve—most of what he was told and had read was correct, but unfortunately *it did not apply to him!*

We now know that using the LAWs model effectively requires an extensive interview that determines the student's flexibility, strength level, injury history, and, most importantly, the body type. (See chapter 3 for tests.) In addition, since concepts cue motor responses, it is very important to find out the student's concept of the swing.

Students do what their concept dictates. At first glance the student who picks the club up and reverse-pivots looks like a bad learner, but if that student's concept is to take the club straight back and straight through while keeping the head down, what you're really seeing is a bad concept combined with good learning skills. Unfortunately, it's a combination that produces a bad swing. The first step, then, is to change the learner's concept, thereby combining the correct concept and good learning skills to produce a good swing.

Barrel Man articulated his concept with ease: "I like Payne Stewart's swing; it's long and powerful and looks beautiful." Now, Payne

Matching the width model puts him in a much better position. His head floats with his coil, and he's in a good position to use his powerful upper body during the downswing.

Stewart measures six-foot-one and weighs about 185 pounds; Barrel Man is five-eight and 190 pounds. Not much of a match there. To make matters worse, someone told him early in his playing career that his swing was too short, even though, after just two years, he was shooting in the high eighties with his self-taught swing.

We began to realize this is a common theme among students. Hearing it so often made it a prime marker which led us to flesh out our matching theory, outlined in detail in chapter 8. Here's the profile: a decent, self-taught athlete who, through trial and error, matches his swing type to his body type and thus produces good results. Because of this success, he becomes more interested in the game and decides to "get serious" by taking some "real" instruction through books, magazines, and/or lessons. The instruction he receives is standard issue, not pegged to his individual characteristics.

Jim Albus, the burly powerhouse who won over a million dollars on the Senior Tour in 1995, is a perfect model for Barrel Man.

He's a very good learner, and he quickly learns a new swing perfectly —perfectly wrong. He now has a swing that is mismatched to his body type and doesn't even know it. Progress comes to a halt, his game falls apart, and he gets mad at himself for being such an oaf. He spends most of his time on the golf course muttering about how hard golf is.

The key for Barrel Man was to change his concept and adopt swing mechanics that would accentuate his strengths and minimize his weaknesses. First he had to ditch Payne Stewart as a swing model. There was no way he could swing the club high and long above him without exceeding his threshold of flexibility. Trying for the long swing caused him to collapse his left arm and raise up as he neared the top of his swing. From this position he could only chop at the ball with a cut-across swing filled with lunges and lurches.

He needed to go back to his short swing, where his left arm stayed straight and his hands moved away from him rather then over him. He also needed to think about producing more width and less height, much like Craig Stadler, Duffy Waldorf, Jim Albus, or John Cook, who are good models for his body type. He moved the ball back in his stance so he didn't have to slide to get to the ball on the downswing, and he changed his left-handed grip to a stronger, three-knuckle position to match the new ball position. He completed his matching by drawing his right foot back and flaring both feet to increase his ability to turn. He also positioned his left arm directly on top of his chest rather than beside it, enabling his arms to swing freely without running into his body.

We know that these swing mechanics contradict the standard, but Barrel Man is not your average golfer. It took a few lessons to put all the pieces in place, but his golf game soon improved dramatically. His comments were much like those we would hear repeatedly in the coming years as we perfected the LAWs model. "It feels so natural, so easy, so comfortable; it feels like it's supposed to," said Barrel Man. That is exactly what happens when your technique matches your physique.

If matching worked for Barrel Man, we theorized, it ought to work for others, from tall, thin, one-iron types to medium-sized, balanced-body types. A good model explains things, and the LAWs model, even in its initial stages, answered questions such as, Why do equally good players on the professional tours have swings that look so different? Why am I a decent athlete in other sports and so bad at golf? Why do I lose my swing so readily, and why does it take me so long to get it back? Why is golf such a hard game to learn and even harder to play? The more we thought about these and a host of other questions, the more the model took shape.

The Framework of the LAWs Model

It's important to note that the only way your club head can take the most direct route to the ball, the power route, is if you match your swing type to your body type. When you do this successfully, you gain access to your dominant power source (DPS). Here's how it works.

A major part of the allure of golf is the distance a golfer can hit the ball. In other ball games, the ball doesn't travel very far. Making a fifty-foot jump shot is a thrill, as is a sixty-yard pass in football. Yet it's merely a 7-iron to hit a golf ball out of the deepest part of Yankee Stadium, a prodigious blow with a baseball for even the mightiest slugger.

THREE POWER SOURCES

Basically, there are three sources of power that you can take advantage of to create distance: mechanical advantage, positional advantage, and muscular advantage. You use all three power sources in varying combinations when you swing the club, but you have a dominant power source that is determined by your body type.

The mother of all errors occurs when you try to access power from dimensions in which you're physically unsuited to operate. When you set up and swing so that you operate in your dominant dimension, you can plug directly into your dominant power source.

1. Mechanical Advantage: The Leverage Swing

Mechanical advantage is arranging your muscles and bones according to the principles of mechanics so that you can move your body in an efficient and powerful way. Levers, such as the ninety-degree angle formed by your left arm and the club shaft, are multipliers of power in your golf swing. As a leverage player, you use the hinging and straightening of levers (your arms and wrists), the stretching and coiling of your muscles, and a tight, centered hip rotation to generate power. David Frost, Chip Beck, Steve Elkington, and most LPGA players are prime examples from the pro ranks.

The leverage swing, also know as the "modern" swing, favors a more modestly built player with balanced proportions. The leverage swing is the simplest motion, creating the fewest angles as the club head rotates around the body.

When the power angles are released, there's some snap in it.

2. Positional Advantage: The Arc Swing

A certain amount of power (energy) is conferred on an object by virtue of its position. For example, if a small stone is dropped from the first floor, it bounces harmlessly off your head. If it's dropped from the hundredth floor, it could go right through you. In your golf swing this is the power of arc—the height and distance your club head travels from address to impact. During the arc swing, the club head moves away from you and then up and over your body. All else being equal, the farther your club head travels, the more powerful your swing

Height is power. An object (like the club head) high above the ground is loaded with potential energy that becomes power in motion during the downswing.

will be. The arc player spends the most time of any player in the height dimension, generating power from an upright swing, with the club traveling on a wide, high arc. Payne Stewart, Fred Couples, Davis Love, Michelle McGann, and Betsy King are all excellent examples.

The arc player is a combination of a swinger and a hitter, with a flowing swing that turns violent as the hands reach impact. The body type best suited to the arc swing is thin-chested and flexible, with long arms in relation to the trunk.

3. Muscular Advantage: The Width Swing

Muscular advantage refers to a player's ability to use physical strength to produce club head acceleration. Muscles generate power by pulling on bones, so the trick is to configure your body so that the big-banded muscles of your back and thighs are in optimum position when they contract. The stronger these muscles are, the more power you can produce, so that all other things being equal, the strongest machine wins.

As a width player, you'll spend much of your backswing pushing the club away from your body while relying on a strong upper-body rotation to deliver a powerful hit to the ball. Craig Stadler, Bruce Lietzke, Duffy Waldorf, and Laura Davies are excellent examples of width players who use their upper torso to good effect. They are players with muscular advantage who smash the ball.

POWER IS A BLEND

While every golfer uses a blend of all three power sources—leverage, arc, and muscles—to hit a golf ball, we all have a dominant power source (DPS), the primary source to which we're most suited. The key is that your DPS is dictated by your body type, and that's where the LAWs of golf comes in.

The width player takes advantage of the sling-shot effect as he stretches the top of his body against the bottom and then releases the pent-up stretch at impact.

POWER LEAKS

We see thousands of golfers each year in our schools and private lessons, and most of them don't hit the ball nearly as far as they could. Why? Because they're asking their bodies to do the impossible. The point is that mismatching your swing mechanics and your body type costs you power. Matching your swing to your body plugs you into your dominant power source and fills the power leaks.

Unfortunately, most golfers are disconnected from their dominant power sources because of mismatching. The greater the power deficiency, the greater the tendency to hit at the ball, adding inaccuracy to power problems. The good player focuses on an even acceleration with no manipulation, while the bad player tries to force acceleration of the club on the downswing. This manifests itself as the "hit instinct"—an overpowering urge that plagues many amateurs.

The standard advice—"swing easier," "slow it down," or "let the club do the work"—just makes matters worse. The club does no work on its own; swinging easier only hits it shorter, not better; and slowing down a bad swing gives you *a slow, bad swing*. So how do you keep your swing powerful? The answer is to plug up those power leaks, which is why we have included a section on power leaks in the leverage, arc, and width chapters.

THE FOUR DIMENSIONS

As far as we know, everything we do in this universe, including playing golf, occurs in four dimensions: the three spatial dimensions of height, width, and depth, along with the fourth dimension—time. How you move your body around in these dimensions determines how well you'll play the game of golf. For example, when your club head takes an indirect route to the ball, you violate the time dimension and arrive at impact either too late, creating a slice or push, or way too early, producing a pull or a hook. In either case, by taking an indirect route to the ball, you leak power along the way, making it impossible to play your best golf.

TIME AND MATCHING

Most golf instruction focuses on what the club is doing in the three dimensions of height (up/down), width (back/forth), and depth (behind). These dimensions are easily observable, and they therefore appear more real and controllable than does the forth dimension—time. And yet time is a huge part of playing the game well. If you hurry your preshot routine, you'll pay the price: you might snatch the club inside on the takeaway and trap it behind you, or you might start down too quickly from the top so your club cuts across the ball at impact. In other words, to swing the club correctly in the three spatial dimensions, you must control your sense of time, a sense we call your "time IQ." Thus, a very important part of learning and then keeping your golf swing is to develop a recognition of your time IQ.

When the club head is high above the body line (represented by the white board), it's in the height dimension; when it's moving away from the body, it's in the width dimension; and when the club head is behind the body line, it's in the depth dimension.

Personalized Time

Many great athletes report the ability to make time appear to stand still, or at least to slow it down dramatically while they are in competition. Jerry Rice, the perennial all-star receiver for the San Francisco 49ers, says when he's at his best, the ball spins so slowly that he can see the writing on it. Reggie Miller, all-star basketball player, describes the zone as a place where everything is in slow motion. He says, "I see plays before they happen, read defenses and know what the defender is going to do before he does it." One of baseball's best hitters, Ken Griffey Jr., says he can slow the pitch down in his mind to give him more time to hit it.

What the Model Is — and What It Is Not

The learning model outlined here is unique because it unifies two things that for too long have been kept separate: swing theory and practical application. Put another way, *it establishes you, the "individualized" student, as the centerpiece of the instructional framework.* The particulars of each swing type and how to match them to your body type will be outlined in the following chapters, but for now it's important to understand the concept of what the model is all about — and what it is not all about.

The model is not a straitjacket method that promotes three swings instead of one. With the LAWs you learn something new every time you use it; the model is alive, dynamic, and ever-changing. It shrinks as hypotheses are discarded and grows when they are added.

But while the LAWs model is grounded in science and experimentation, it is not dogmatic; it is merely a framework within which you learn to realize your golfing potential. It is a road with signposts that provides a starting point and a destination — a fairly definite image of what your swing will look like at the end of your journey. But it is the journey itself that is the true creative act, promoting the art of learning.

Models vs. Methods

A model is a general representation of a theory that helps to promote further study of the relationships between certain key variables that make the model work. Models are made up of intertwined, complementary hypotheses that cohere or hang together without contradicting one another. If one hypothesis is proved false, it can be discarded without destroying the model. Models are organic, alive and ever-changing as new evidence is presented. Models, such as the LAWs of golf, enhance the creativity of both the learner and teacher.

Before the LAWs of golf, no model existed that explicitly outlined how you choose the right combination of swing mechanics as you set about to satisfy the three controlling factors of the game of golf: the laws of physics, the rules of golf, and your physical characteristics. What does exist and what has been the basis for most golf instruction is a group of methods: hard-nosed, stone-carved edicts, each purporting to apply to all golfers. In reality, these methods disregard the importance of individual differences in body structure, flexibility, and physical strength, and are therefore of limited effectiveness.

There are many ways to go from New York to Los Angeles, and all of them will get you there, but as a traveler you have to know something about your trip. You have to know about your starting point, New York, even if that means knowing only how to get out of town—and you have to want to get to LA enough to keep you going. You also have to have a method of transportation: are you going to fly, drive, or walk? And, among other things, you have to know when you've arrived; otherwise you'll end up in the ocean.

If learning your golf swing is a journey, you have to know where to start and where to end, because at some point you have to put aside swing mechanics and models and go play golf. Some of you will fly, some will drive, and some will have to crawl, but if you want to get there, the LAWs can help you.

To effectively use the LAWs model, we recommend the following:

1. Identify your body type (chapter 3).
2. Adopt the set of swing mechanics best suited to your type (chapters 4, 5, and 6).
3. Learn your LAWs swing by using specially designed drills, teaching aids, and exercises (chapter 7).
4. Customize your LAWs swing by studying ball flight and using the LAWs matching theory (chapter 8).

Chapters 4, 5, and 6 outline the model with descriptions of the setup and swing characteristics for each of the three basic swing types as well as the power leaks that trouble each type. This classification highlights the differences between the leverage, arc, and width swings, but to fully understand these differences, especially the more subtle ones, you should first understand the characteristics essential to all swing types and all good golf swings.

Similarities in All Swing Types: The Three Pivot Points

Unless there's an injury, the body uses three major pivot points to execute the golf swing: the spine and the two hip joints. Regardless of body type, each swing type has three rotational centers that create the possibility of the movement known as the golf swing. For the purposes of classifying each swing type, however, we have labeled each swing in accordance with its predominant use of one of these pivot points. So while each swing uses all three, each uses them differently to get the job done. These differences are quite obvious in appearance — hence the following labels.

Because of limited flexibility, the width player has some lateral movement of the upper spine in order to pivot successfully, first around the right hip joint and then the left. In this case, for the purpose of classification, we describe the width swing as a two-pivot swing (right and left hip). The arc player keeps the upper spine fixed, and since that is a basic difference in usage, we call this a single-pivot swing. The outstanding characteristic of the leverage swing is a rotary look, with very little lateral motion. It gives the appearance that the golfer is using all three pivot points equally, so we designate this as a three-pivot swing.

An important note: there is a difference between a pivot center (a cluster of points), a pivot point, and an axis of rotation (a straight line), but with a muted apology to physics, we often use them interchangeably. We also use imprecise terms such as force, power, speed, and so on, the type of acceptable inaccuracies that get the job done in the vernacular and are not meant to have the precise meaning they have in science. This text is not designed to explain the physics of the golf swing; it seeks rather to help you play better golf. In certain instances, where the distinctions make a significant difference, however, the appropriate terms are used.

The Takeaway:
A Forty-five Degree Arm Swing

For every swing the hallmark of an ideal takeaway is the left arm swinging forty-five degrees across the chest to complete the takeaway. When the left arm is in this rock-solid position, it provides a perfect blend of connection and leverage. For a player with an average chest size and a moderate amount of flexibility, this forty-five-degree standard is achieved almost automatically because the left arm can only swing so far before it reaches its full extension. We term this "running out of left arm." But since chest sizes differ, the LAWs model provides setup positions that allow players of different builds to achieve the same goal.

For example, the width player—whose large chest and minimal flexibility limit his arm swing—bends more from the hips to allow the arms to hang directly downward and over the chest. From this configuration the left arm can swing uninterrupted to forty-five degrees. On the other hand, the arc player, whose thin chest and high flexibility can cause excessive arm swing, stands more upright so that his arms have less freedom of movement and can swing only forty-five degrees. Your chest size, then, acts as a governor that limits how far your left arm can swing on its own. The thicker or more protruding your chest, the sooner it stops your left arm from creating the correct angle.

Moving Through the Dimensions

The most important dimension in the takeaway for all swing types is width. No matter what the swing type, the end of the takeaway is accomplished once this forty-five-degree angle is established. At the end of the takeaway, however, the body types show marked differences. At this point the club head peels off into the respective dimensions depending on swing type: height for the arc player, additional width for the width player, and depth for the leverage player.

Blending Arm Swing and Body Turn

In all swings there's so much up and down motion and so much around motion. A good swing is a perfect blending of the two in which the arms do the up and down and the body does the around. It's vital that they stay with their appointed task and don't get into each other's business.

When you're mismatched, this allocation of duties is misassigned. If the body gets into the business of the up-and-down and/or the arms get in the business of the around, you can't take the most direct route to the ball.

You can see the role that the arms and the body play exemplified in the swing of Fred Couples, an arc player who, according to most experts, "picks the club up" during the backswing. All he's really doing is letting his arms do the up first and then, just before he reaches the top of the swing, his body adds the around. There's a different sequence to the blend, but both his body and his arms stick to their appointed tasks, producing the correct blend of the up/down and around.

Once the takeaway is finished, the club head peels off into the player's dominant dimension: depth for Leverage; height for Arc; Width for the muscular-advantage player. Note that because of the Arc player's late wrist cock, the club head is still almost even with the hands. It is about to soar high above him.

HANDS SEPARATE FROM THE RIGHT SHOULDER

It is a characteristic of all swings that your hands must separate from your right shoulder at some point in the downswing.

By the time your left arm is parallel to the ground, your right arm begins to straighten, catapulting your club head away from you into the width dimension. Thus, you drop the club head and widen your club-head arc while retaining the ninety-degree angle between your left arm and the shaft.

The Most Direct Route to the Ball

For all swings the key to consistently good golf shots is to find a position at the top of your swing that gives you the most direct route to the golf ball so you can arrive at impact on the shaft plane

Here the arms have followed the body rotation and are too far behind the player.

angle established at address. To do this, your body and swing type must match. All swing types, when the swing is executed correctly, are either on or very close to being on the shaft plane established at address by the time the club shaft is pocket high, just before impact.

In all swings some movements are sequential (first this, then that) while some are simultaneous. *When* the movements occur is as important as the fact *that* they occur.

Find Yourself in the LAWs Model

So where do you fit in the model? You'll find the answer in chapter 3, where you can find yourself in the model and then use the information in subsequent chapters to build your blueprint based on the guidelines that apply to you. It is important to note that the general guidelines that follow must be adjusted and fine-tuned to your individual characteristics. Knowing you are an arc player, for example, is only the starting point. You should begin by following the model exactly, but once you've adopted the correct swing mechanics for your body type—the appropriate grip, stance, takeaway, and so on —it's time to begin the process of customizing your swing *within your swing type*. This should be done, we believe, under the watchful eye of a certified LAWs instructor, but this book will go a long way in helping you.

Before you begin your customization, we recommend that you read the entire book and then reread chapter 8, which contains the

The tour player Mike Hill maintains his power V (right arm bend) until just before impact. The straight left arm over the bent right arm is a common configuration for expert golfers.

LAWs matching theory, where you'll learn which swing specifications blend beautifully and which mix like oil and water. We like to say that what is magic for one is tragic for another. This way you'll know exactly where the boundary lies, and you won't go down the blind alleys that create so many golfing Frankensteins.

3

Finding Yourself in the Model

In most sports the athlete matches his or her body to the demands of the game. In a sense the sport chooses the athlete. In track and field, sprinters have muscular, well-proportioned bodies; marathoners are lean and slight; and shot-putters are heavyweights with large chests and very powerful thighs. At a sports dinner there's no mistaking an NBA center for a jockey, and you won't confuse the sumo wrestler with the motocross champ. Elgin Baylor, the Hall of Fame forward for the Los Angeles Lakers, was asked by a waiter at a late-night diner if he and his teammates were pro athletes. His reply has become a classic: "Yeah, we're midget wrestlers."

In golf, however, there are no sport-specific requirements: both Corey Pavin and Ernie Els are world-class players, as are Laura Davies, Rosie Jones, Chi Chi Rodriguez, and Jack Nicklaus. But even though golf is open to all body types, success does depend on a matchup of another kind: how well you match your technique to your physique.

The LAWs model has much in common with models used in other fields that use body types and other classifications to make sense of the world. Here are a few of the more famous models. Most, like the LAWs model, use tests or other techniques that allow individuals to locate their place within the model.

Indian Philosophy/Medicine. Prakriti is Sanskrit for "nature" or "body type," and it tells the practitioner of traditional Indian medicine which diet, physical activities, and medical therapies you should use. There are three basic operating principles: the Vata, the Pitta, and the Kapha. Body types are inherited—they're the mold you're cast in. Knowledge of this allows you to evolve toward the perfect match; violation of it drives you toward a mismatch, the ultimate cause of sickness.

Diet Based on Body Types. This system classifies people according to which of the four major glands is dominant in their body: the pituitary, the thyroid, the adrenal, or the gonadal. Each gland represents a specific body type, and the model outlines what foods you crave and where fat deposits appear on your body. Although all glands influence every type, one gland exercises dominance and direction. The dominant gland has the greatest influence on your appearance—specifically, your body shape and fat distribution. The G type puts on weight in the rear end, the A type in the stomach; the T type is slim/skinny, while the P type gains weight all over.

The Chinese Typology. This system classifies body types according to which of the five elements is dominant in the body: earth, fire, water, air, or ether.

Yin and Yang. This is the binary division of two basic types of energy or forces present in people. According to this Chinese theory, there are two forces in the universe representing the duality of nature: yang, the male side, represents heat, light, heaven, and dominance; yin, the female side, represents cold, dark, earth, and passivity. This theory suggests that a wise person will recognize these forces in every area of his or her life and maintain balance by regulating the two.

Freudian Theory. Sigmund Freud, the father of psychoanalysis, identified the famous threesome of the id, ego, and superego. According to to Freud, these three shapers of behavior operate as a system of checks and balances for human behavior; imbalance among the three breeds neurotic behavior.

While there is a dominating force in each of these theories, nobody is all yang, all thyroid, all fire, all Pitta, all superego, or, in the case of the LAWs model, all leverage, arc, or width. Models such as these, no matter what the field is, contain the idea that human beings share the same elements but differ based on the blending of these elements. *The successful person is correctly balanced*—eating the right foods for one's hormone mix, doing the job that fits one's energy type, cultivating compatible relationships with one's partners in marriage and business. And *in golf, matching the swing to one's body type.*

Body Types and the LAWs

In 1940 the sociologist W. H. Sheldon created a scale dividing the general population into three prototypical body classifications: endomorph, mesomorph, and ectomorph. The scale is a one-to-seven rating system based on how many characteristics of each prototype a person possesses. While it recognizes most people as hybrids with a blend of traits, the triadic classification is useful for the identification of general types.

Within and across the three types, there is much variation in characteristics such as size, strength, and bone structure, all of which determine how someone will perform an athletic motion such as the golf swing. We incorporated these three body types as the foundation of the LAWs model, then outlined three basic swing types—leverage, arc, and width – that match the three body types.

Body Type	Body Characteristics	LAWs Swing Type	LAWs Body Type/ Swing Type Match
Mesomorph	Balanced	Leverage	Leverage player
Ectomorph	Long-limbed/ Thin-chested	Arc	Arc player
Endomorph	Short-limbed/ Rounded	Width	Width player

NOTE: *Throughout the rest of the book, rather than constantly referring to the mesomorph, and so on, we've taken the liberty of describing them as types of players: the leverage player is the mesomorph; the arc player is the ectomorph, and the endomorph is the width player.*

While the laws of physics are uniform, it is obvious from the outline above that the people who exercise these laws are not. Some are evenly proportioned, with wide shoulders on a medium-size skeletal frame. A well-conditioned mesomorph is muscular, with a triangular-shaped upper body, much like Greg Norman, while the average mesomorph has less definition and a little more body fat, like Steve Elkington. We refer to individuals with builds like this as leverage players and recommend they begin the matching process using the leverage swing.

Other people are tall and thin-chested, with long, angular features. Tiger Woods and Davis Love are prototypical ectomorphs. We label individuals of this body type as arc players, who, not surprisingly, should use the arc swing. The third group, the endomorphs, are thick-chested, often with short arms and limited flexibility. They are powerful players who can be muscular like Craig Parry and Hal Sutton, or very large-chested, with a higher percentage of adipose tissue like Laura Davies and Craig Stadler. This body type is suited to the width swing, and we refer to people who exhibit this type as width players.

Identifying the LAWs Types

It's this natural fit between body type and swing type that makes the LAWs so powerful, although we hate to use the word "natural" because it's so overused in golf today—as if there were some innate wiring in your DNA that, once activated, brings out the swing that's waiting within you. Language is innate, and human logic is, too, but golf is not. Your golf swing not only must be learned, it must be matched to you, and no amount of coaxing will draw it up from within; it must be put in from without.

We believe that if a beginner with some talent were marooned on a desert island with an endless supply of range balls, a 5-iron, and unlimited trail and error, he would develop into a good ball striker. Eventually he would find the swing that suited his body and allowed him to satisfy the laws of physics. The desert island is a necessity in this case because no one would be around to preach the latest theory or the "right" way to swing a golf club. No one would be there to tell him that his swing looked too long, too short, or too "leggy." The beginner would simply find what suited his body and satisfied the physics of the golf swing. Beyond that, right and wrong wouldn't exist and his ignorance would lead to blissful golf.

The good news is that you don't need a desert island, though you might need to clean the slate concerning your view of right and wrong. With the LAWs model our goal is to outline the basic swing that is best suited to your body type. Then we'll guide you through a process of customizing your swing so you can create a blueprint based on your unique physical characteristics and the nuances of your swing.

THE BODY TYPES

The photo on page 32 shows four golfers from left to right: a leverage player, of medium build; a tall and thin arc player; and two varieties of short and stocky width player, one with a large chest and broad shoulders, the other of more moderate size. Our entire thesis can be summed up in one sentence: *According to the LAWs model, each golfer must swing the club differently because each has a different build.* This is logical, but is it true? To answer this question, let's take a closer look at our models.

SWING HEIGHT

The plane and height of a golf swing differ based in part on the distance from a person's forearm to upper arm. In the photo on page 33, you can see that when the width player folds the right forearm, the thumb falls below the shoulder line, which indicates that his swing plane will be flatter and lower than the other two players' swings. The arc player's thumb is well above his shoulder, so he'll have a high and upright swing plane. The leverage player's thumb arrives level with his shoulder, so his swing plane will fall between the two extremes.

The prototype body types are, from left to right: leverage (mesomorph), arc (ectomorph), and two types of width player (endomorph), W1 and W2.

ARM SWING

The amount that each player can swing his left arm in the backswing also differs based on chest size. We recommend that all golfers swing their left arm about forty-five degrees across their chest during the takeaway to maintain connection and to give the club head sufficient width. When the width player swings his left hand to meet his right, his arm runs into his chest well before his hands meet. But by bending more from the hips, the width player can increase his arm swing to forty-five degrees. The leverage player's left arm runs into his chest at the same time his hands meet, so he naturally has the right amount of arm swing from a standard golf posture. The arc player can swing his arm excessively because of his thin chest, so his posture will be more upright to limit his arm swing to forty-five degrees. In the following chapters the specific posture adjustments are outlined for each swing type.

The length of the forearm in relation to the upper arm influences the height of the hands at the top of the swing.

SHOULDER FLEXIBILITY

The path of the club head will be affected by the amount of flexibility in the shoulder joints. The width player can't rotate his right forearm to the perpendicular position, so his right side will tend to work out and around during his downswing, and he'll fight coming over the top. To match his swing to his body's capabilities, he'll close his stance and move the ball position back. This allows him to come over his body line, back onto the target line during the downswing.

The arc player has no trouble rotating his arm back past his shoulder. In fact, because of his flexibility, he's always in danger of swinging too far behind him. This traps the club and causes him either to come over the ball and pull it or to leave his shot to the right. His takeaway and the lateral hip bump protect him from this tendency. The leverage player's right forearm stays straight up and down; assuming his swing is sound, his arms will therefore drop directly down to the ball using the most direct route.

Here the models demonstrate the effect that chest size has on arm swing: the bigger the chest, the more restricted the arm swing.

The Letter of the LAWs

We've used the LAWs Identification Tests (LIT) to help thousands of students identify their body types. Your body type might seem self-evident to you, but you can be fooled if this is the only way you judge yourself. The more you tend to be a blend of two types—that is, the more you look like a hybrid, as most do—the more each question will help you find yourself in the model and customize your swing within the framework of the LAWs. So to discover the nuances of your body type, our advice is that you answer every question because this will help you to better build your complete golf swing blueprint from the LAWs model.

Many questions have three choices, some ask for ratios or actual measurements, and others ask for your opinion. Don't agonize over your answers—this is not an IRS form. And please remember that

This player has dropped the club into the "pro slot" and because his right elbow is in front of his right hip, he can deliver the club head to the ball on time.

like all testing of this type, the conclusion is built from an accumulation of its parts, one by one. In other words, while no single question or answer can classify you, the weight of all your answers will give you a strong indication of where you fit in the LAWs model.

NOTE 1: Most women are leverage players, but if you are a woman who has some unusual characteristics—for example, if you are very strong or have a large chest—then go ahead and take the test, adjusting it where necessary.

NOTE 2: Consult your physician before you attempt any of the tests or exercises in this book.

THE BODY RECOGNITION TEST

The Body Recognition Test is often the most accurate available. It simply involves looking in the mirror. Obviously there are numerous combinations of characteristics that we call hybrids. You can be short and weak, stocky and very flexible, or tall but with limited flexibility.

To refresh your memory, the three prototypes can be described as follows:

1. A medium-framed mesomorph with arms and legs in proportion, giving the appearance of symmetry. Moderately flexible and may have fleshy areas but in general is of average build with a medium height/weight ratio (for example, five-foot-nine and 155 pounds). This is the profile of the leverage player.
2. A small-boned, thin-chested ectomorph, often tall with long limbs in relation to the torso. Usually very flexible, and with a high height/weight ratio—for example, six feet and 155 pounds. This is the profile of the arc player.
3. A large-framed, big-boned endomorph, with a thick chest and short, powerful legs and arms. Fleshy with both fat and muscle evident in some proportion. Usually not very flexible. The tendency for this body type is a low height/weight ratio (heavy for their height)—for example, five-foot-eight and 180 pounds. This is the profile of the width player.

Depending on how much you look like one of these body types, rate yourself as follows:

Leverage body type: L
Arc body type: A
Width body type: W

Your letter of the LAW is _____

ARM ELEVATION TEST

Stand against a wall with both shoulders blades touching the wall. Allow your arms to hang beside your body, and make a pistol of your right hand with your thumb in the cocked hammer position. Keep your right elbow against your rib cage, and fold your right arm up toward your shoulder. Now measure the relationship of your

The pistol folds up below the shoulder, so this player gives himself a W.

thumb to your shoulder. If your thumb is above your shoulder, score yourself an A; if your thumb is about level with your shoulder, give yourself an L; if it folds below your shoulder, score it a W.

Your letter of the LAW is _____

ARM SWING TEST

Touch your shoulder blades to the wall and extend your arms directly in front of you horizontal to the ground just like the models in the photo on page 34. Now swing your left arm across your chest and stop *as soon as* your upper arm runs into your chest. If it stops before your hands meet, score it W. If your hands meet as your left arm is stopped by your chest, score it an L. If your left hand moves past your right hand before your left arm runs into your chest, record that as an A.

Your letter of the LAW is ____

SHOULDER FLEXIBILITY TEST

Enlist the aid of a friend to anchor your shoulder, or place your right shoulder blade against a door frame. Bend your elbow ninety degrees with your upper arm, and elevate your right arm so that your elbow and shoulder are level (as if you were taking an oath). With your shoulder fixed, rotate your right forearm back. If you can't rotate your right forearm until your elbow is perpendicular to the ground, give yourself a W. If your forearm stops at or just slightly past vertical, record that as an L. If you can rotate past vertical, give yourself an A.

Your letter of the LAW is _____

HIP/LOWER BACK FLEXIBILITY TEST

Before you do this or any other exercise, warm up your muscles. When you take the test, be sure you don't strain or bounce your muscles in an effort to exceed your flexibility level.

Lay two clubs on the floor perpendicular to one another. The X club is the one between your legs, while the Y is along your heels. Adjust them so that the point where the clubs intersect is marked by the beginning of the grip of the X club. Sit on the floor with your legs fully extended about ten inches apart, positioning the Y club across your heels so that the X club is between your legs. Now, without bending your knees, lower your head and gently reach as far as you can along the grip of the X club.

If you can't reach the grip, give yourself a W; if you can reach past the point where X and Y meet, give yourself an A; and if your reach extends somewhere along the grip, score an L.

Your letter of the LAW is _____

ROTATIONAL FLEXIBILITY TEST

Stand against a doorjamb so your club won't hit the wall when you turn. Make sure your feet are parallel and shoulder-width apart. Lay down three clubs as benchmarks: club one parallel to and touching

Ignore the hand position, and rate yourself only on the forearm position. Here the model's forearm is straight, and he gets an L. With less bend, give yourself a W; if you can bend more, your letter of the LAW is an A.

This test gives important information about your hip flexibility that will be used in chapter 8 to customize your swing.

your left foot; club two extending from your right heel across your left toe; and club three running from your right toe parallel with the second club. Now anchor your rear end firmly against the wall with both cheeks touching. Your head should also be anchored and your posture in the military review position with shoulders back, head up, and eyes forward. Take a fourth club and place it across your chest about three inches below your throat. Keeping everything firmly pressed against the wall except your shoulders, rotate from left to right as far as you can.

If you're short of or just barely making it to club one, give yourself a W. If you make it easily past club one but stop about halfway between club two and three, give yourself an L; if you make it past

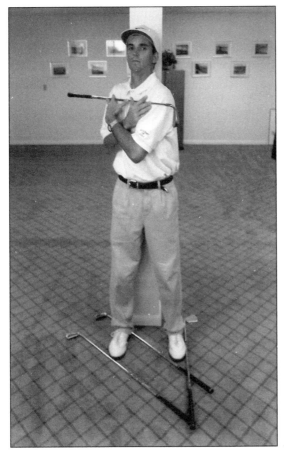

This test gives you information about your upper-body rotational flexibility.

the halfway point, you get an A. Remember, cheeks and head don't leave the wall.

Your letter of the LAW is _____

THE DOMINANT DIMENSION TEST

As we have already seen, finding your dominant dimension is closely linked to your body type. Big-chested, short-armed golfers don't do well swinging the club high above them, and tall, flexible types shouldn't try to swing the club around behind them. One way to determine your dominant dimension is to match yourself to our three models.

As demonstrated on page 42, stand in your golf posture, and swing only your right arm to the top of your backswing; hold that position. Now bring your left arm up to meet your right arm, keeping your address posture and your left arm straight. To determine your dominant dimension, match your look with our model golfers. As you can see, the width player has a large gap between his hands and must bring his right arm down to his left to unite his hands and restore his golf posture. His hands meet in the width dimension with his left arm below his shoulder.

If you have a gap like this, give yourself a W. The arc player has no gap, and his hands meet in the height dimension, with his left arm pointing above his shoulder line. If this is your match, write A as your score. The leverage player has no gap either, and his hands meet very comfortably in the depth dimension, with his left arm and shoulder line matching. If you do the same, your score is an L.

Your letter of the LAW is _____

YOUR HEIGHT

Short: under 5 ft. 8 in. = W
Medium: 5 ft. 8 in.–5 ft. 11½ in. = L
Tall: 6 ft. plus = A

Your letter of the LAW is _____

This test shows the major effect flexibility and chest size have on your dominant dimension. The width player can't reach up to connect his arms, so he must bring his right arm down, out of the height dimension, to meet his left. The arc player easily reaches his right hand, while the leverage player's reach is lower and farther behind him.

YOUR BONE STRUCTURE/FRAME

NOTE: Here is one way of determining your frame size, as adapted from the Metropolitan Life Insurance Company charts. With your fingers straight and your palm facing your side, bend your right elbow to ninety degrees. Using your other hand, place your thumb and index finger on the two bones that stick out on either side of your elbow, and record the distance between your thumb and index finger. Use the chart below to match up height and frame size. If you're below the number for your height, you've got a small frame; if above, a large one. If it's in the range listed, you're normal.

Height in 1-Inch Heels = Elbow Width

5'4"–5'7"	=	$2^5/_8$" to $2^7/_8$"
5'8"–5'11"	=	$2^3/_4$" to 3"
6'–6'3"	=	$2^3/_4$" to $3^1/_6$"
6'4" plus	=	$2^7/_8$"+

Large frame = W, medium frame = L, small frame = A

Your letter of the LAW is _____

YOUR WEIGHT

Height & Weight Table for Men

Height Feet Inches	Small Frame	Medium Frame	Large Frame
5'2"	128–134	131–141	138–150
5'3"	130–136	133–143	140–153
5'4"	132–138	135–145	142–156
5'5"	134–140	137–148	144–160
5'6"	136–142	139–151	146–164
5'7"	138–145	142–154	149–168

(continued)

5'8"	140–148	145–157	152–172
5'9"	142–151	148–160	155–176
5'10"	144–154	151–163	158–180
5'11"	146–157	154–166	161–184
6'0"	149–160	157–170	164–188
6'1"	152–164	160–174	168–192
6'2"	155–168	164–178	172–197
6'3"	158–172	167–182	176–202
6'4"	162–176	171–187	181–207

Weight at ages 25–59 based on lowest mortality. Weight in pounds according to frame (in indoor clothing weighing 5 lbs. for men and 3 lbs. for women; shoes with 1" heels)

Overweight = W, medium = L, underweight = A

Your letter of the LAW is _____

SHAPE

Match your shape to the graphics.

Round or square = W
Pyramid or triangle = L
Cylindrical or tubular = A

Your letter of the LAW is _____

HEIGHT/WEIGHT RATIO

Use the continuum to locate your ratio

Height/Weight Continuum
(Calculated in Inch/Pounds)

◄── Higher───────────	Medium ───────────	Lower──►
0.48 ratio	0.41 ratio	0.35 ratio
74 in. / 155 lb. = 0.48	72 in. / 175 lb. = 0.41	66 in. / 190 lb. = 0.35

Your rating:
Low H/W = W; medium H/W = L; high H/W = A

Your letter of the LAW is _____

CHEST SIZE/HEIGHT RATIO

Divide your chest size by your height in inches. For example, if you have a 40-inch chest and stand 68 inches, 40/68 = .58 ratio—a leverage body type.

.66 to .62 — high ratio = W
.61 to .55 — medium ratio = L
.54 to .51 and lower — low ratio = A

Your letter of the LAW is _____

YOUR NECK SIZE

Large—16 in. plus = W
Medium—15 in. – 15$^1/_2$ in. = L
Small—15 in. and less = A

Your letter of the LAW is _____

YOUR WAIST SIZE

Large—36 in. plus = W
Medium—32 in.–35 in. = L
Small—32 in. or less = A

Your letter of the LAW is _____

SLEEVE LENGTH

Short—less than 32 in. = W
Medium—32 in.–34 in. = L
Long—35 in. plus = A

Your letter of the LAW is _____

PANTS LENGTH

Short —less than 32 in. = W
Medium—32 in.–34 in. = L
Tall—35 in. plus = A

Your letter of the LAW is _____

ARM SPAN TO HEIGHT

Fully extend your arms at shoulder height, and measure from your right index fingertip to your left and compare that measurement to your height. If your arm span is longer than your height, give yourself an A; if they match, record an L; and if your arm span is shorter than your height, write down a W.

Your letter of the LAW is ____

YOUR OVERALL FLEXIBILITY LEVEL

Low = W
Medium = L
High = A

Your letter of the LAW is _____

This completes your List. Now simply add up your letters:

W's _____ L's _____ A's _____

YOUR OVERALL STRENGTH LEVEL

Ws (strong), Wm, (medium strength), Ww (weak)
Ls, Lm, Lw
As, Am, Aw

Strength level _____

Once you know your swing type/body type match, rate your overall strength as strong, medium, or low, and put it in the appropriate space. So if you come out as an arc player and you're a strong person, put As in the space. If you're a weak width player, write in Ww. You'll use this information later as outlined in chapter 8, when it is time to customize your swing.

If you're still not sure what you are by using the letter of the LAW test, here is some advice. The most important single physical characteristic that influences the swing types is flexibility. The second is the chest size/height ratio. Also important is your strength level, your height/weight ratio, and the overall shape of your body.

If your flexibility is width (check out your letters of the LAW regarding flexibility), go to the width section. If you're very flexible, with not much of a chest in relation to your height, and your height/weight ratio is high, you're an arc player. If you're moderately or highly flexible and you look like a leverage player and have the chest/height ratio of a leverage player, you are one. We're often asked in what category we'd place a golfer who is tall, muscular, perfectly proportioned, and very flexible with a lot of strength. The answer is the superstar category, such as Ernie Els, Tiger Woods, and Greg Norman.

Below is a complete outline of the LAWs ID system:

Triangular	Cylindrical	Round or Square
Symmetrical proportions	Long limbs	Short levers
Medium to high flexibility	High flexibility	Low flexibility
Medium chest	Thin chest	Thick chest
Medium height/weight ratio	High height/weight	Low height/weight

4

The Leverage Player

PROFILE

Body type: mesomorph

Distinguishing feature: level hip turn

Dominant dimension: depth

Dominant power source: mechanical advantage

Swing motion: rotational

Overall look: whirling

Finish position: side bow (side C)

Shaft load profile: two bursts

(TOP LEFT) *The leverage player is in a perfectly balanced posture with the top of the spine, shoulders, tip of the elbows, knees, and balls of the feet in alignment. The lower leg is properly straight rather than angled forward.*

(TOP RIGHT) *The backswing begins with a simultaneous movement of the left arm swinging across the chest and the right hip turning back over the right heel. The shaft is parallel to the target line with the toe of the club pointing to the sky.*

(BOTTOM) *The arm swing pulls the chest and shoulder behind the ball as the right arm folds and elevates the club, keeping it on the swing-plane angle.*

He arrives at the top of the back-swing with his hips level and his left arm at the same angle as his shoulders (relative to the spine), a perfect, on-plane position. His club face and the back of his left hand are also matched for a square club face.

The club is dropped into the slot by the arms and the lower-body action, which is cued when the left hip turns back over the left heel. The angles formed by the club shaft and arms are maintained insuring a powerful release of the levers.

(OPPOSITE TOP LEFT) *Just after impact the shoulders have opened slightly to the target line, and the hips have turned much more, to about forty-five degrees. He's flat-footed and rotating.*

(TOP RIGHT) *He has maintained his spine angle as his body has fully released through the shot.*

(BOTTOM) *The finish is balanced. Note the slight curve of his body to the right: the side C position of the leverage player.*

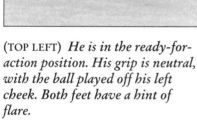

(TOP LEFT) *He is in the ready-for-action position. His grip is neutral, with the ball played off his left cheek. Both feet have a hint of flare.*

(TOP RIGHT) *At the end of the take-away, he has already set the angle between his left arm and the club shaft. This early creation of this angle (the left-side leverage) is characteristic of the leverage player.*

His left knee and hips are resisting the coiling of the upper body. This is a modern swing, with very little hip turn early in the swing. Note that the legs have not moved at this point, although weight has transferred to the right hip.

(OPPOSITE TOP LEFT) *The right elbow fold elevates the club, and the right wrist cups to set the club head in the depth dimension. Finally, we see some left-leg motion, but the hips have still not turned very much, so the coil continues to build.*

(TOP RIGHT) *At the top of the backswing, his upper body is fully coiled against his lower body, with both feet firmly on the ground. His right wrist is in the tray position, supporting the club. Again, notice the level hips and the width he maintains between his knees.*

(BOTTOM) *The downswing begins with three separations: the weight shifts to the left hip, separating the legs; the hands separate from the right shoulder, slotting the club; and the left shoulder separates from the chin. Both feet are flat on the ground, but his weight is shifting rapidly to his left hip.*

(TOP) *Just after impact both arms are fully extended, a result of a complete and unrestricted release of the club head. Note the firmness of the wall formed as his left leg straightens, allowing the energy to transfer fully into the back of the ball.*

(BOTTOM LEFT) *It is only now that his right foot is pulled off the ground as he continues to rotate through the shot. This is a perfect example of the modern rotational swing in which the bottom of both feet stay looking at the ground through impact.*

(BOTTOM RIGHT) *He finishes with the chest facing slightly to the left of the target and the right shoulder closer to the target than the left.*

General Description

The leverage (L) swing favors a modestly built individual with balanced proportions. The body of the leverage player remains level and flat-footed throughout the swing, with the hips, knees, and shoulders maintaining their positions relative to one another as they rotate around their respective axes. The leverage swing has a whirling look because the club moves around the body, and the dominant dimension is depth.

The L player delivers the club face to the ball on a very direct route and is therefore an accurate player. There is not much lateral movement of the hips as the upper body stays centered around the spine as it rotates. At the end of the takeaway, the right arm folds and elevates the club to the shoulder plane and then unfolds to start the downswing as it drops the club down the shaft plane—all while quietly rotating around its three pivot points: the spine and the two hip joints.

In the downswing the weight shifts to the left hip, and the arms drop downward. Once this shift/drop is underway, the turn back to the ball occurs. The left hip reestablishes the pivot point as it turns back over the left heel while the arms drop downward. Once this movement is completed, the right side turns to the ball.

The leverage swing employs mechanical advantage, utilizing the hinging and straightening of levers and a tight, centered hip rotation to generate power. Because of the efficient use of levers, there are no excesses in height, width, or depth. In what has come to be known as the modern swing, this flat-footed, compact motion incorporates a body release. The hands have a notably passive look. The shoulders are level to the inclined spine as they turn, not level to the ground. In the L swing, the club is never forced off the swing plane angle. The player who maintains his levels while he swings simply slides the club up the plane angle as the right elbow folds and back down again as the elbow straightens. This is the ideal route for combining power and accuracy because it is so direct.

The swings of David Frost, Chip Beck, Steve Elkington, Jeff Maggert, and most LPGA tour players are good examples. Because this swing type creates very few unnecessary angles between the golfer, the ball, and the target, the swing is a very low-maintenance one, requiring the least practice. The human eye doesn't like oblique angles, such as those created in Jim Furyk's or Miller Barber's swing, and since the leverage swing is on the plane angle all the way through, it looks symmetrical. It's the one the TV announcers call "a simple swing" because that's the way it looks to the eye.

The Particulars of the Leverage Swing

TASK 1: SETUP

Your setup writes the script for your golf swing. A proper setup encourages good balance as well as correct swing mechanics; an improper setup is the cause of most swing flaws no matter what your swing type. We estimate that over 90 percent of all swing errors are caused by a faulty setup. We define the setup as grip, ball position, posture, stance, aim, and alignment.

Grip. The purpose of the grip is to guarantee control of the club without inducing tension. When the hands are applied correctly, no manipulations are necessary to return the club face square at impact, nor is there need to consciously use the wrists. A good grip activates the muscles you want to use in the golf swing; an incorrect grip leads to the use of the wrong muscles.

As an L player, take your grip in the following manner: extend your arms and hold the club at a forty-five-degree angle in front of you, with the heel pad of your left hand on top of the handle. This places the club across the top joints of the fingers (where the fingers meet the hand). The heel pad supports and traps the club, relieving you of the need to hold the club in a death grip. Golfers—especially beginners and intermediates—who place the club on the ground and then take their grip, often position the club too diagonally in their hand so that it is lodged too high in the palm.

Hold the club at a forty-five-degree angle in your right hand, and place the handle across the finger joints where the fingers meet the palm.

By placing the grip under the heel pad, you also free your wrists to hinge properly throughout the golf swing. Use a *medium-long left thumb* to promote the setting of your wrists. To encourage the correct thumb length, take your grip with your arms fully extended in front of your chest, and close your left hand around the club handle. You should find that your left thumb falls slightly to the right of the top of the handle and that your wrist is square to the club face. This positioning is important because when centrifugal force straightens your arms through impact, your wrist joint, elbow joint, and shoulder joint will align. Therefore the club face must be set at address to prepare for the inevitable alignment of those joints. (Note: ignore the markings on the grip—they are not meant as guides for your hands).

The heel pad, marked by an X, anchors the club, allowing control without inducing tension in the grip. Note the medium-long thumb.

If the anatomical snuff box located at the top of your left thumb is to the left of the center of the shaft (in a weak grip position), centrifugal force will cause the club face to arrive open at impact. Conversely, if the snuff box is to the right of the center of the shaft (in a strong position), the club face will arrive closed at impact. Since the hallmark of the leverage swing is its simplicity and lack of compensatory moves, the left-hand position is vital.

Place your right hand on the club so the palm faces your left palm. Your left thumb fits in the channel formed by the heel and thumb pad of your right palm. Arranged in this way, your right hand is directly behind the handle, aligned with the club face and square to the target line. The pressure points are in the last three fingers of both hands. Once your hands are set on the club, you can check to see if your right hand is correctly placed simply by extending your right index finger down the shaft. If your index finger extends down the side of the shaft so that the shaft is between your index finger and the target, you're in good position. If your index finger extends either on top or underneath the shaft, the right hand isn't in the correct position.

For the woman leverage player, the left hand is more on top of the grip in a strong position.

When your grip is correct, you'll have it firmly in your control without the need for tension. If you strangle the club, you'll cut off all feel for the weight of the club head, making it impossible to cock your wrists correctly. If you grip the club too lightly, your brain will sense it and, at some point in your swing, you'll regrip the club to maintain control. On a scale of one to ten where ten is very tight, your pressure on normal shots should be in the five range. To prevent your grip from becoming a weak link in your swing, assimilate the procedure outlined here so thoroughly that it becomes an unconscious element of your preshot routine.

Ball Position. There are three ball positions, depending on what club you're using. To be sure your ball position is correct, we avoid references at ground level. Ball position should be based on the upper body, which provides a more stable checkpoint since it is easier to monitor.

For the L player the following ball positions apply: for the 5-iron through the sand wedge, position the ball off your left cheek; when you're playing a long iron (1–5) or a fairway wood, move the ball about one ball width farther forward between your left cheek and underarm; for your driver or other woods on a tee, it's off your underarm.

Golf is a game of geometry, and the correct ball position is vital to facilitate the rotary action the leverage player needs to make a powerful and accurate swing. One way to look at it is that all you're really doing with your setup is arranging a collision, so that when your club head arrives at the appropriate point on the arc, the ball simply gets in its way. If the ball is somewhere other than the ideal position, the impact will be mistimed.

Ball position also influences your shoulder alignment and, consequently, the path of your swing. Position the ball too far forward and your shoulders open. This encourages the out-to-in swing path characteristic of a slicer. Position the ball too far back, and your shoulders close, promoting the in-to-out path that can produce a hook.

To use these guidelines effectively, make sure your head is positioned in the center of your body and your eye line is parallel to the intended line of flight. Since your head serves as a reference for correct ball position, tilting it will distort your view. In addition, correct eye alignment is important because there's a tendency for the swing path to follow the eye line. Your hands should swing away on your toe line for a proper leverage takeaway, but most golfers who tilt their eye line to the right at address swing the club too far inside during the takeaway. Those who tilt left often make the opposite error—an outside-the-line takeaway.

The ball doesn't move very far, but it must move about a ball width to adjust for the varying lengths of your clubs.

Posture. The way you stand to the ball determines in large part how easy it is to swing the club in your dominant dimension. This athletic position stacks the load-bearing joints in alignment so that your muscles will be ready for a quick, powerful movement. Correct posture allows you to create maximum velocity consistently. To do this you need pivot points that produce the whirling power of the leverage player.

Each sport has its characteristic starting position: the quarterback taking the snap, the tennis player receiving a serve, the defensive back in the ready position—and the proper posture for the leverage golf swing. When your spine is inclined correctly, it creates room for you arms to swing, and it lines up the joints. You should be able to draw a straight line from the top of the spine through the tip of the elbow and from the tip of your knee down through the ball of your foot. From the face-on view, you'll see the major load-bearing joints—your shoulder, hip, knee, and ankle joints—stacked atop one another in their strongest, most stable position. This stability allows good balance throughout the swing.

You create this posture by bending forward the same amount as you bend from the hip sockets back from the knees. Most amateurs make the mistake of forcing the knees forward over the balls of their feet, leaving the upper body too erect, blocking the arms from swinging correctly, making it difficult to turn the hips, and thereby ruining in-swing balance. Check your lower leg to make sure that it's

The ready, athletic position with the club shaft at ninety degrees to the spine.

straight up and down from sky to ground; if it's slanted, your knees are too flexed.

Weight distribution also affects balance. For maximum balance, your weight should be distributed from the balls of your feet to your heels. The top of the spine, the tips of the elbows, and the balls of the feet are in alignment, and your knees bowed out over your ankles to help create balance.

Your feet should be flared the same amount and *square* to the target line. Maintain an upright spine angle (no tilting toward or away from target) without hunching your shoulders. Your chin should be up in the proud position, and your rear end should jut out as if you were about to sit on a medium-high stool. Flex your knees in the ready position to discourage any up-and-down body motion. If you prepare yourself correctly, you won't have to make any adjustments once your swing begins.

The spine is your upper-body pivot point, the axis around which your upper body turns. The correct posture also arranges the club shaft and spine at ninety degrees to each other. This is an important angle because an object swings fastest when it's perpendicular to its axis and will always seek 90° to its axis. If your spine is too vertical, centrifugal force will pull the club head out toward the target line, causing an out-to-in swing path.

Stance Width. The narrowest foot width occurs with the short irons; for these clubs your heels are hip-width apart. The widest stance is for your driver; for this club your heels should be about shoulder-width apart. The rest of your clubs are somewhere in between. The measurement is always taken from the middle of your heels, never from your flared toes.

To check your heel width, take the appropriate stance for the club you have chosen; without moving your feet, reach behind you and mark the middle of each heel with a tee. Now take a club and, using your thumb as a marker, measure the width of your shoulders or hips, depending on which club you are using. To make sure your stance width is correct, compare the width you have marked on your club shaft to the distance between the tees on the ground. Use this procedure periodically to check your stance width.

The width of your stance influences your stability, balance, and mobility. Another way to check your stance width is to turn into your follow-through position; if your knees reach each other, your stance is the correct width. If your knees can't reach each other, your stance is too wide. If they overlap, your stance is too narrow. Too wide a stance causes a reduced hip turn and encourages excessive lateral motion, while too narrow a stance causes a reverse weight shift.

A Square Stance. "Creating the square" shows the geometric relationships between your body, the club face, the ball, and the target line. When we use the term "square," it means that your shoulders, hips, knees, and feet are all parallel to the target line.

Lay down four clubs in a square. One represents the target line, and one represents your foot line (those two are parallel); the third runs down your right heel to form a perpendicular with the target line; and the fourth extends from your left heel and is also perpendicular to the target line. The four clubs form a square in relationship to the target line. When your body is parallel with the target line, its said to be *square* to the target. When your club face points to the target, it is also square.

Aim/Alignment. The key here is to begin all normal full shots from a square setup position with regard to both your club face and your body. And since it's your club face that makes contact with the ball, the direction in which it's pointed at impact will determine the direction the golf ball will travel. It's helpful for aiming to use the lines on the toe and heel of your club face. It may sound simplistic, but you must take great care to aim your club face at the target at address, because that's where you want it facing at impact.

The alignment of your hips is important because your hips dictate the amount of rotation away from and back to the ball. Open hips cause you to turn too little on the backswing and therefore they point too far to the left of target. If your hips are closed at address, you run the risk of turning too much on the backswing and then not being able to get your hips turned back in time for impact. With your leverage body type, square hips at address give you just the right amount of turn back and through.

Since your shoulders determine the direction in which your arms swing, the shoulders must be aligned correctly to insure that your club face looks at the target at impact. Your shoulders should be parallel to the target line because your arms swing in the direction that your shoulders point. When you're aimed to the right, your swing path is too in-to-out, and the reverse is true when you're open.

Foot Flare. The amount of hip and shoulder rotation during your backswing depends on how flexible you are; you can regulate this rotation by the amount you turn your feet out at address. The less flexible you are, the more flared your right foot should be to allow you more turn. The more flexible you are, the less your right foot should be flared to prevent you from turning too much.

By itself, your foot position is the least important of the body alignments but is one of the most important for power transfer. At impact, the left leg must act as a wall to create a transfer of energy at the bottom of your arc. Therefore it's vital to arrange your left leg and foot so that at the moment of impact, there's a sudden and very powerful transfer of energy from your club head to the ball. This is why you need to customize your foot flare to your body build.

The Backswing. To help you learn the backswing effectively, we have divided it into two parts: the takeaway and the loading zone. In the takeaway your club swings away on your toe line until your left hand is an inch or so past your right foot. At this point your left arm is fully extended, a position signaling the end of the takeaway that we call "running out of left arm." The second part of the backswing is the loading zone, which is roughly the area from the end of the takeaway and the top of the swing. It's where you set your angles of leverage and develop the ratio of coil that gives your swing its power.

TASK 2: THE TAKEAWAY

There are two things that you need to do during the takeaway, and they happen simultaneously. Your left arm must swing across your chest as your right hip begins to turn over your right heel.

The left arm swings to a forty-five-degree angle for maximum power, because during your downswing it stays melded to your chest so the full force of your body is behind the club. By creating this angle during your takeaway and keeping it intact during your backswing, you've established the correct downswing position. Simultaneously, your weight shifts into your right hip, establishing your right side pivot point as your right hip turns over your right heel. Be careful here because it's possible to turn your right hip without putting load in it, a common mistake that leaves the weight in the left hip, creating a reverse pivot: you've turned your hips but your pivot is wrong.

Neither your chest nor your shoulders should turn until they are pulled around by the left arm as it swings away from the ball—the sequence being arm, then shoulder, then chest. At no time, then, is there any slack in your backswing—slack breeds slap, a looseness in the backswing that causes a weak slapping action through impact because of a lack of coil. By swinging the left arm to create maximum stretch, you keep tension on the muscles constant, which leads to a powerful release of this tension at impact. Also, the more stretch you create, the wider your swing arc will be, which means more club-head speed and power.

Now you don't consciously prevent your chest from moving, but you condition it to wait for the left arm tug, a signal that comes as soon as you "run out of left arm." The sequence of motion led by the left arm keeps a stretch on the muscles of the left side of your body, especially your triceps. This is the beginning of coil, and to maximize it keep your shirt buttons even with the ball until the pull of your left arm swing becomes irresistible.

Allow your right elbow to float, which will open a *window* between your elbow and your right side. If your elbow stays against your side, your club will pivot around it, taking the hands inside the toe line, a difficult position to recover from. The key to your takeaway is to keep the club head outside your hands as your hands move along the toe line. Allowing the right elbow to float prevents the hands from moving inside the toe line.

When waist high, the left arm and wrist are still straight, and the club is parallel with the ground since it hasn't been elevated by the

The window shown here (space between elbow and body) is a key leverage feature. The leverage swing is very rotational, and the window keeps the arms from simply following the body as it turns.

wrist cock. In other words, none of the height the club head has attained so far is due to wrist cock. From here the arms stay close to the body, and the club is set in position at the top of the swing by your right arm folding and your coil motion.

TASK 3: LOADING

As an L player, you want your club head and shaft down the toe line and parallel to the target line at the end of the takeaway. From here your elbow fold is both upward and backward, positioning the right hand deeper than your right shoulder, much the same as when you throw a ball.

The Wrist Set. When you set or cock your wrists, you create an angle (usually ninety degrees) between your left arm and the golf club. The club sets in response to the momentum of the swinging club head and the folding of your right arm. Your right wrist bends back toward your forearm, thereby creating wrinkles across the top of the right wrist, a most important move that keeps the club on the shaft-plane angle created at address. The bending of the right wrist sets the club on the shaft-plane angle. Thus the club is set correctly without the hands being drawn inside the toe line during the take-away, a move that often causes the error commonly referred to as "over-the-top."

The left wrist angle increases as the club swings away along the toe line. As the right wrist hinges, it causes the left wrist to cock upward (creating wrinkles at the base of the left thumb), giving height to the club head. The key to the L takeaway is *low hands, high club head*; any other combination, such as low hands/low club head or high hands/high club head, results in an off-the-plane angle position. The arms continue to swing back and up, causing the shoulders to turn on an incline at right angles to the spine (the spine is the axis for the shoulders).

Once your takeaway is completed and your wrists have set cor-rectly, all the relationships you need to complete your backswing are in place. All you have to do now is to continue your arm swing, which will turn your shoulders and create the coil. The shoulder turn completes the backswing by carrying the club to the top of the swing. The right hand supports the club in the "tray" position at the top, and the left heel remains planted, creating the necessary coil to initiate the downswing. Shifting your weight into your right hip joint establishes the backswing pivot point. The hips turn level to the ground because you have retained your knee flex. Level hips and knees are indicative of the L swing.

Note that at the top of your swing, your elbows are level with each other and a triangle is formed by that level line and your fore-arms. This triangle contains two important relationships: your left arm forms a ninety-degree angle with your club shaft (which makes up the left side of the triangle), and your right arm, by bending at the elbow, creates an angle (ninety degrees for the L player) that forms the right side. For descriptive purposes we'll call the former *the left-side leverage* and the latter *the right-side leverage*. As we shall see in the next section, when and how you release these two sides deter-mines the quality of impact.

The Downswing. Your downswing is divided into two parts: the slotting of the club that places your club on the correct path and the delivery zone where the power built up in your body is transferred to the ball.

TASK 4: TRANSITION AND SLOTTING

As your left hip turns over your left heel, your left arm begins its slide back down your chest, maintaining constant contact as the club drops downward. By the time your left arm is parallel with the ground, your right arm *begins* to straighten, catapulting the club head away from you into the width dimension. Thus, you drop the club head and widen your club-head arc while retaining the ninety-degree angle between your left arm and the shaft (the left-side leverage).

To start the downswing, your club must move down before it moves forward toward the ball. The only way this can happen correctly is if your triangle drops straight down, and this means that your hands must move away from your right shoulder. This is what we mean by the term *separation.* Thus your hands and right shoulder should never move together. Note that while the width player can tolerate the hands and right shoulder moving together to reposition the club onto the target line, the L player cannot.

In addition to your club dropping, your downswing is initiated by filling your left hip joint with load (weight), thereby establishing the left-side pivot point and preparing the lower body for rotation and power delivery. A word of caution: leaving your weight in your right hip too long during the downswing causes fat shots or pull hooks, so don't hang on your right side.

A common problem for the L player is getting off the right side too soon, with the right hip releasing outward toward the ball. Your right cheek needs to stay against an imaginary wall until it's pulled off its mooring by the left hip clearing to the left. This opposition between the left and the right sides of the body, one pulling and one resisting, creates a second level of coil by ratcheting up the tautness of the coil you built in your backswing. As we'll see in more detail in chapter 6, this coiling produces the bandy-legged position so evident in the swings of leverage players.

The hip action is the most misunderstood part of the leverage swing. At the beginning of the downswing, the left hip is prepared for rotation when you deposit weight in it, but the right side doesn't rotate to the ball until the arms drop the club head into position. At this point the knees separate as the left knee follows the left hip, while the right leg resists the pull of the left side.

TASK 5: DELIVERY ZONE

Once your left arm has dropped the club into position and you've established your left hip joint as your pivot center, you're prepared to release your right side. At this point your left side is ready to act as a buttress or wall of resistance against which you will hit. The right side stays back as the left shoulder moves out from under the chin, and the arms drop the club downward into the delivery zone. The club must move down and then around— never around and then down. It is very important that the arms drop the club down the shaft-plane angle before the club moves forward. Once this is done, your right side rotates back to the target, thereby delivering the club face squarely to the target at impact.

The key here is that while your left side, from the knee down, stops to form the wall that you hit against at impact, your entire right side must continue moving so it can smack full force into that wall. This collision gives you a powerful, well-timed release. The concept that cues the right side of your body during your forward swing is that *everything that is moving should keep on moving.*

As a leverage player, you use a body release with minimal independent hand activity. Your arms stay close to your body throughout the swing, and the left foot remains on the ground. The L swing is characterized by a very tight, centered rotary motion that delivers energy at impact with a straightening of the levers.

TASK 6: THE FINISH

For the flexible leverage player, the right shoulder often ends closer to the target than the left, with the chest facing left of the target. You should finish with most of your weight on your left side, with the front of your body facing the target, using your back foot as a rudder. Your upper body is upright but tilted a bit to the right, with the right shoulder slightly lower then the left (sideways C or bow). The club shaft finishes behind your head on a line that runs through the ears, but since the head is tilted slightly, the club shaft is diagonal with the ground.

The Advantage of the Leverage Swing

Golf is played best with a minimum of angles and a maximum of arcs. There is an optimum-approach path of the club that allows the energy to be delivered from club to ball directly at the target rather than down into the ground or up into the sky—a U-shaped swing with a flat spot at the bottom of the arc that levels out through impact, rather than O-shaped (too rounded) or V-shaped (too steep). The leverage player can swing the club head around himself without changing levels and without getting the club head trapped behind his body. This swing provides a perfectly balanced approach angle—not too steep and not too shallow. It is a whirling action around the body using a three-axis swing, the two hips for the lower body, the spine for the upper body.

Women and the LAWs

One reason women don't hit the ball as well as they could is exactly the same reason men have trouble with the game—they're mismatched. Historically, women were taught theories and methods developed with a man's body as the prototype, but this is not true of the LAWs model. The physical differences between all golfers are considered, and the swing mechanics are adjusted to fit those differences. In general, women have more flexibility, less muscular strength, especially in the upper body, and a lower center of balance than men.

MODIFICATIONS OF THE LEVERAGE SWING

Although women could benefit from the power of the arc swing, most don't have the upper-body strength this swing type requires. A long, high arc is great way to produce distance, but only if the club is in control. When the club is out of control, the swing produces off-center hits at impact, which doesn't sound like too much of a problem until you consider the following: strike a ball only a half of an inch outside the sweet spot (the center of the club face), and you can loose 7 percent of your total distance. Using the average length drive for women of 130 yards, that's almost a 10-yard loss. Thus an out-of-control arc swing only magnifies the distance problems.

The muscular-advantage-style width swing is also not a good choice for women because the short club head arc doesn't supply enough power unless it's matched with upper body strength.

With a few exceptions like Michelle McGann, Beth Daniel, Betsy King, and Sally Little (arc players), and Alison Nicholas and Laura Davis (muscular-advantage players), most women golfers, professional or amateur, should use a leverage swing. Within the general guidelines of the LAWs model, the following are specific recommendations based on the level of upper-body strength, flexibility, and distinctive body contours of the women golfer.

SWING ADJUSTMENTS CAUSED BY PHYSICAL DIFFERENCES

On Your Toes. When it comes to the knees, studies show that women are the weaker sex. The width of the pelvis results in a sharper angle where the bones of the upper and lower leg meet (the knees), thereby creating alignment problems for the kneecap. Women's ligaments tend to be more flexible than men's, but while men's hamstring muscles are usually very strong, women's are not. Women therefore rely more on the stronger quadriceps muscles (front of the thigh) to stabilize the knee than the hamstring muscles located behind the thigh. This may be one reason why many women's heels come off the

Tour player Sally Little is an exception—a woman who is an arc player. She is as close to the prototype as there is. Note how the angle of the left arm is more vertical than the shoulder angle.

ground during the downswing. Although there are some very fine players (like Laura Davies and Tiger Woods) whose heels elevate, this is in large part a response to very high club-head velocities, something that most players don't have to worry about. For the average player, moving weight toward the toes and raising both heels during the downswing is counterproductive. If your heels come off the ground at impact and you're not generating a lot of distance, we recommend that you do exercises to increase the strength of your hamstring muscles.

To be sure you're distributing your weight correctly, practice hitting balls with your toes curled, a procedure that will force you to distribute your weight from the balls of your feet to your heels during your swing. At first you may feel as though you're rocking backwards as you near the top of your swing, but that's just because you're used to being too far up on your toes.

The Overswing. Women tend to be more flexible than men in their hips and knees, which makes it easy for them to turn their hips too much in the backswing, causing the club to swing too much around and behind the body. If you're flexible and you swing way past parallel, position your right foot perpendicular to the target line even though you're a leverage player. This limits your hip turn but allows the upper body to turn; when you turn your shoulders more than your hips, you build coil.

Another reason many women swing the club past parallel is because the left arm bends during the backswing; instead of turning the shoulder behind the ball and setting the wrists early to support the weight of the club, then simply lift the club up with the arms and hands without coiling. This is one reason why the one-piece takeaway is not for you. In this case it won't do you any good to point your foot at the target line—in fact, it could make things worse.

While women often have very strong leg and thigh muscles, their upper-body strength is limited, especially in the forearms and hands. Therefore, you have to focus on releasing your forearms by aggressively rotating them through impact. Many women don't allow this rotation to occur because they hold the club in a death grip and guide it to the ball. So much tension and energy is exerted to steer the club that the natural and powerful release of the club face through impact is inhibited. You ought to be able to grip the club lightly enough so that you don't immobilize your wrists. It's helpful to squeeze a tennis ball and do some forearm curls to increase the strength of your release muscles.

The Grip. Women have a tendency to misposition the club too high in the palm of the left hand because they usually take their grip with their left arm at the side of the chest, with the club head resting on the ground. Since the club shaft is diagonal to the body in this position, it's very easy to position it too high in the palm of the left hand as you reach down to take your grip, a flaw that might cause you to lower your right shoulder too much as you reach under to grip the club with your right hand.

To avoid grip problems, use the following procedure to grip the club: with your right hand, hold the club in front of your chest at a forty-five-degree angle to your body. Extend your left arm out to meet the club, making sure your left upper arm is resting on top of, rather than beside, your chest. Position the club in your left hand so that your heel pad is on top of the grip and the side of the grip (which faces the target) runs in a straight line along the top finger joints of your left hand. Close your hand and extend your left thumb as far as you can down the right side of the shaft. This "long left thumb," characteristic of the width player, will serve you well because it maximizes wrist cock and helps support and control the club at the top of the swing.

Next, holding your club with your left hand, hover your right hand over your left hand, and then lower it onto your left thumb so that it fits into the channel formed by the fat pad and thumb pad of your right hand. Putting your right hand on the club from above assures that you will hold the club in the fingers of both hands.

Thus, your grip is strong in the left hand (the back of the left hand is pointing toward the sky) but more neutral with the right (the palm of your right hand is facing the target). Once you've taken your grip, you can check it by simply extending your right index finger down the shaft. If it lines up directly behind it so that the shaft is between your finger and the target, you're fine. If the finger is on top of the shaft, your right-hand grip is too weak; if it's under the shaft, it's too strong.

You can take a giant step toward having the correct grip pressure by making sure you grip the club more in the fingers of your hand rather than deep into the palms of your hands, as described above. This allows your wrists to relax so they can cock and produce leverage.

While your grip style—overlap, interlock, or ten-finger—is largely a matter of preference, we prefer the overlap grip for women with above-average strength and the ten-finger for women of average to below-average strength. With all ten fingers, it allows you to cock your wrists more easily, increasing leverage and helping the release.

Posture and Setup. In keeping with the theme of the LAWs model, chest size is an important feature. Women of average to large breast size should set up with their left upper arm resting on top of their breast. This position allows women to keep their left-arm-to-chest connection, a vital element of all good golf swings. When the left arm is placed beside the breast, the arm has to swing out and around, and you lose connection with your body. When the left arm rests on top of the breast, the left arm can swing as it should, unimpeded during the backswing.

In the leverage swing, the goal is to bend enough at address to allow forty-five degrees of arm swing during the takeaway. And depending on the size of your chest, you'll bend progressively more from the hips for a larger chest, less for a smaller one.

If your chest is medium to large, you might need to bend more from your hips to position your left arm on top in order to increase your spine angle and create space for your arms to swing the club. Because of the increased spine angle, your head (which weighs about ten pounds) will be "hanging" out over the ball, obliging you to stick out your tailbone as a counterbalance. For reasons of propriety, some women are hesitant to do this, but this posture is necessary for good balance. It prevents the top part of your body from pulling the bottom from its moorings during the swing.

Because of your flexible shoulders you need a wider stance than the leverage model recommends. This allows your shoulders to turn more than your hips in order to create coil.

Ball Position. In a good swing the club head approaches impact slightly open, squares to the ball on contact, and then closes after the ball is gone—a natural progression when you consider that the club is swung in a sort of tilted arc. Since your grip is strong, the club face closes earlier in the impact zone, obliging you to play the ball about two inches back of the standard L position.

Turn vs. Coil. Many women are loose-jointed, with a good deal of flexibility in their shoulder and hip joints. This characteristic makes it easy for them to turn while they swing, but it does not necessarily mean that they create coil. It is important for all golfers to remember that there is a turn in every coil but not a coil in every turn.

Coil occurs when you turn one part of your body (the top) against another (the bottom), using the big-banded muscles of the back and hips. This coiling is converted into club-head acceleration. Women who turn everything together (knees, hips, shoulders, and chest) actually turn too much, preventing coil and creating a huge loss of power.

The LAWs model takes the foregoing into consideration by giving you special drills and teaching aids (as outlined in chapter 7) that teach you to coil correctly.

Here the player is turning too much, rotating her hips and shoulders the same amount and producing very little coil.

This is a coiled position in which the hips resist the shoulders.

The Swing Itself

Create a Window. Remember that you have a strong grip with your left hand and so it's important not to let it turn your right arm behind your body too early in the backswing. During your takeaway your right elbow moves straight back from the ball (not behind your body) the same amount as your left arm moves across your chest. This creates a window of space between your upper body and your elbow.

Light Is Probably Right for You. One way to maintain control of your club is to make the club "light." You might not always be aware of it, but the pull of gravity is a constant force that affects everything you do, including how you swing the golf club. When you swing the club up and away from the ball, your club travels against gravity, and it takes a certain amount of exertion on your part to overcome it. To feel the effect of a "heavy" club, try the following experiment: using your sand wedge, make a one-piece takeaway so that your club shaft extends down your toe line horizontal to the ground. Now stop with your hands about waist high and both arms fully extended. Hold this position for sixty seconds while monitoring how the club head becomes progressively heavier.

Now make the same arm swing during the takeaway but let your wrists cock before your hands are waist high so that the shaft is upright and slightly tilted with the club head pointing behind you. Hold this position for sixty seconds and compare the two feelings; the first was heavy, the second is light.

As we have said, you must be physically strong to use the one-piece takeaway characteristic of Payne Stewart and Michelle McGann, where the chest, shoulders, arms, and hands turn as a unit as the club moves away from you. The problem is that if you're not strong enough, your brain will sense it, and you'll simply lift the club with your arms instead of turning and coiling it to the top of your swing as you should.

Since you don't want to struggle with a heavy club, use a takeaway with an early set or cocking of the wrists that maneuvers the club into its lightest position very early in the backswing. This way you can rely on shoulder turn rather than on arm lift to bring the club to the top.

A Simple Answer to the Distance Problem. The LAWs model does two basic things for the woman golfer: it puts the club under your control, and then it gives you the go-ahead to grip it and rip it.

Many women simply don't swing hard enough, some because they can't. Women who swing with very low club-head speed often do so because trial and error with a weak grip taught them that the faster you swing, the more it magnifies the problem. As the swing got slower, the ball flew straighter, but distance progressively dimin-

Using a one-piece takeaway makes this club very "heavy."

ished. We recommend that first you get your technique correct and then force yourself to swing more aggressively.

If you're just beginning, you should emphasize distance more than accuracy. If you learn accuracy first, you probably won't ever become a long hitter. It's much easier to swing hard and learn to control it later. If you've been playing for a while, get out of the habit of steering the ball. Remember that the club won't do the work for you—you have to do it. Put another way, "Grip it (correctly) and rip it."

Keep the Right Side Moving. A big power leak for women is that in an attempt to guide the ball to the target, they don't keep the right side moving through impact. But when your right side stops or slows down in the middle of the downswing, it causes a weak slap at the ball with the hands and arms. The proof is evident at the finish of the swing, when the right knee points right of target, the hips are almost parallel to the target, and a lot of weight is on the back foot.

Leverage Power Leaks

GRIP PRESSURE

Levers are multipliers of power, and the leverage player lays the groundwork for a powerful swing when the left arm and club shaft form a ninety-degree angle during the backswing. The key to power is retaining this angle until just before impact. But when your grip pressure is too tight, you can't cock your wrists enough to form this lever, so all you can do is make a weak slap at the ball.

With the correct grip pressure, your brain, guided by information from pressure sensors in your body, will make the adjustments necessary to maintain the correct hold on your club as you swing. All this is done automatically by your neural networks, high-tech brain technology that comes with every brain. When you strangle the club, you cut off all feel to your brain.

So relax your hands—make it a "hold" rather than a "grip." The hands are clamps, not for crushing but for anchoring. Your grip pressure should be light enough to allow you to cock your wrists, but heavy enough to secure the club in your hand so you don't have to regrip during the downswing. On a scale of one to ten where ten is the tightest and one is the loosest, your hold on the club should be a five. The correct grip pressure allows your wrists to cock (never roll) in the up/down direction, producing leverage that can be released on time. This is the definition of a good grip.

A MISSING COIL

In the correct leverage swing there's a tight, rotary coiling action where your legs resist the turn of your hips and the hips resist your shoulder turn. Thus, there are actually three levels of coil, and, if done correctly, the amount of coil is ratcheted up as the backswing progresses from the first coil (lower legs) to the second (hips) to the third (shoulders).

A primary power leak for the leverage player occurs when the left foot leaves the ground and the left knee buckles and moves out toward the ball. Remember, it's stretch that creates this first level of coil, when you set the lower leg against the hips, and if you miss the first coil, you can never make it up. To get the feel of the first level of coil, assume your golf stance with all your weight on your left leg, using your right toe as a rudder for balance. Keeping your weight planted where it is, rotate your body until you feel the sensation that your left heel is trying to move in the direction of the target. This resistance in your lower leg is the feeling you should have all the way through your leverage backswing.

THREE SEPARATIONS

Once the power is generated, it must be saved for impact. Starting your downswing, three separations need to occur *simultaneously* or coil is lost and power leaks away. Your hands separate from your right shoulder and move directly down toward the ground, maintaining the ninety-degree angle with the shaft. *At the same time* your left hip turns back toward the target while your right hip stays put, creating a separation between your legs. The third separation is the left shoulder moving away from the chin, a move that aids in dropping the arms and the club into the slot. If your left hip turns first without the arm drop, you'll deliver a weak, swiping hit. If your arms drop without the hip turn, you'll release most of the coil way too soon, producing a powerless arm slap; when the left shoulder pulls back off the body line, the club is pulled across the ball, resulting in a weak slice.

STANCE

As a leverage player, the quality of your swing depends in large part on your ability to rotate back and through the ball with level hips. The platform that supports this rotary motion is your legs, so they must be strategically arranged. If your stance is too wide, with your

By letting the left heel raise so far off the ground and the left knee get so close to the right, he's lost his first level of coil and with it his power. Contrast this with the leg position in the photo on page 55.

heels spread outside the width of your shoulders, it's hard to make a good hip turn. In this case wide may feel powerful—but it isn't.

Please do the following experiment, and you'll see what we mean: take your normal setup, and then spread your feet as far apart as they will comfortably go. Now try to make a hip turn, and you'll feel, in exaggerated form, how too wide a stance can be restrictive—unless you have a lot of Elvis in you, your hips will sway instead of turn.

When your hips sway during your backswing, your right hip slides outside your right foot. Once this happens, the potential to build coil is lost along with another important element: balance. Basically, if you don't turn, you tilt your upper body because once your hips have slid out from under you, your head acts as a counterbalance as it moves to the left, tilting your entire upper body back toward the target into an ugly position called a "lumbar reverse." To make matters worse, your upper body tilts toward the target to serve as a counterbalance.

So now, how do you like your wide stance? Your hips swayed while your shoulders tilted, and your prospects of recovery are not good.

But too narrow a stance is no bargain either. Please do the opposite of your "too-wide" experiment, narrowing your stance until there is barely any space between your feet—and for good measure, also turn your feet in toward each other. It's hard to turn unless you leave your weight in your left hip, which is what's known as a reverse pivot because your weight is in the wrong hip, just the reverse of where it should be.

Now it's about to get worse, because you're headed for the double-reverse pivot. When you're on the wrong hip (left) on the backswing, it's pretty common, unless you like falling down, to shift your weight to the right hip on the downswing— again, just the reverse of where it should be.

So take our advice and avoid the agony of "de-feet" by making sure your stance width is correct.

FANS

When you incorrectly rotate the club face it's called a fan, and for reasons not entirely clear, fans can appear out of nowhere to plague perfectly normal leverage swings that are purring along quite nicely. One day you're fanless, and the next day there it is, a squatter in your takeaway. Perhaps it's the focus on being rotary that suddenly creates an impulse to rotate everything you can: arms, hands, the whole works. In any case, fans are power sappers because they spin your club face open, creating the need for a steep, cut-across downswing to close the face. Once you experience the weak slapping action through impact, you'll agree that fans like this you don't need.

Although there are others, the two we'll talk about are the left-hand fan and the left-arm fan.

The left-arm fan occurs during your backswing when your left arm lifts off the chest and creates a gap that breaks your arm-to-body power connection. When your left arm stays against your chest (as it should) but your left hand and your forearms roll (as they shouldn't), you've got yourself a left-hand fan.

Fanning usually means that the club face will be open at the top of your swing (toe pointing to the ground). The left-arm fan also makes it easy to overswing because without your chest to block it at the appropriate point, your left arm can swing out of control. Now, as you start your downswing, your club shaft is steep, and your right shoulder has to work over the top to close the open club face—unfortunately, since you've lost your arm-to-body connection by fanning the club, there is nobody behind the shot. This not-so-dynamic duo—an early release and an off-center mishit—is not the combination you want at impact.

Of course this isn't the whole story, because sometimes the fan can cause the face of your club to be shut (looking at the sky) at the top of your swing. Unless you like to hit rip hooks, you'll have to do your best chicken wing through impact, holding off your release with a megaloss of power.

Rolling your wrists during the takeaway spins the club face out of position.

Adjusting the Model to Fit the Individual

As we will see in chapter 8, most leverage players are not exactly like the prototype, so here are some adjustments to the leverage model based on individual differences. (For a general theory of matching, see chapter 8.)

LOWER BODY

Level hips are important for a level hip turn, so a leverage player whose right leg is longer than his left closes the stance by the amount of the difference to level the hips.

A leverage player who is naturally bowlegged should position the feet to point straight ahead so that the hips and knees are aligned one over the other. A leverage player who is knock-kneed should flare both feet out to align the hips and knees in a balanced, neutral position. (Find the optimum amount of hip turn using the club drill in chapter 7, and then adjust from there).

A leverage player who is naturally left-handed but is playing right-handed will require a stronger right-hand (more under the handle) grip to offset the left side's urge to dominate the swing.

GRIP

Hips that turn quickly should have a stronger left-hand grip to square the club face at impact. Slower hips need a weaker left-hand grip to square the club face. The grip also complements the type of release used—either a body release for fast hips or a more hand-oriented release for slow hips. How the hands are positioned determines how the left wrist angle is set during the initial stage of arm swing. Fast hips need an increased dish angle (the cupping of the left wrist), while slow hips have no cup in the back of the left hand from takeaway to impact.

WRIST COCK

The right hand helps to control the shaft plane going back—when it's placed more on top of the handle, it creates more of a vertical wrist cock; when it's more under the handle in the strong position, a flatter wrist cock is the result. The wrist cock is earlier for slow hips because of right arm fold and later for fast hips.

BALL POSITION

The leverage ball position is adjusted farther back for fast hips to square the face when the player uses a strong grip. The ball is positioned farther forward for slow hips to square the club when the player employs a weaker grip than recommended by the model. Such positioning also helps to speed up or slow down the arms: moving the ball back for fast hips allows the arms to reach their impact position sooner. It has the opposite effect for a forward ball position.

FOOT POSITIONS

For fast hips, both feet have more flare. This creates a greater distance for the hips to turn and delays the straightening of the left leg while keeping the right hip and knee from coming over the top (a tendency for a fast-hipped leverage player). For slow hips, the amount of flare in the feet is reduced, shortening the distance the hips have to travel to impact and once again synchronizing the hips and arms.

POSTURE

Fast hips require a more bent-over posture that creates a steeper shoulder turn and a shorter, more upright swing. An upright plane gives a direct route to the ball that speeds up the arms to coordinate them with the quicker hips. Slow hips require a more erect posture to work the hands farther away from the ball on a flatter plane and to keep the hands longer in the depth dimension, thereby slowing them.

ARM-SWING TYPE

There are three types of arm swing in the leverage backswing that help to coordinate hip speed and arm swing for the leverage player:

1. For fast hips, the left triceps is swung across the chest, in turn swinging the right arm in a wider arc, increasing the cup angle of the left wrist, and keeping the club head outside the hands during the takeaway.
2. For slow hips, the top of the left biceps is swung across the chest, a motion that flattens the plane and decreases the cup angle in the left wrist.
3. For moderate-speed hips, the middle of the left biceps is swung across the chest. This maintains the cup angle in the back of the left wrist.

The arm swing separates the elbows during the backswing. The left triceps across the chest separates the elbows the most, about shoulder width apart. The top of the left biceps across the chest separates the elbows the least.

HAND POSITION AT TOP OF SWING

Fast hips require more direct hands that don't have to travel as far to impact. Slow hips match hands that are farther away at the top. The larger the window, the higher the hands finish at the top; the smaller the window, the lower the hands finish at the top.

CHEST SIZE

A thin-chested leverage player will have a more erect posture to limit the left-arm swing to forty-five degrees. A thicker-chested leverage player requires a more bent-over posture. If you have to bend over to a point that disrupts your balance, then you'll have to close your stance until you're back in balance. As in all the swing types, leverage players need to experiment with their posture until they find a position that permits forty-five degrees of left-arm swing without sacrificing balance.

ARM LENGTH

Unless their clubs are custom-fitted (which we highly recommend), leverage players with long arms will need a more erect posture and should pull their shoulders back (both adjustments will shorten the arms) to a point where the butt end of the club points to the navel. A leverage player with short arms should create more knee flex to get the club back to the ball while bending forward more from the hips. The final adjustment will be to slope or roll the shoulders forward. These adjustments allow leverage players to get down to the ball and swing the club more conventionally.

A narrow-hipped leverage player will require a wider base (stance) for balance and will have slightly more lateral hip motion to promote a good weight transfer. A leverage player with a long trunk will have a more erect posture. His takeaway will be more one-piece, and his swing will be more upper-body-oriented.

Strength and leg length affect how early or late the leverage player sets the golf club during the backswing. The stronger player and the player with longer legs will need to set the club later in the back-swing, creating a more upright position to match what the lower body does in the downswing. The physically weaker leverage player will tend to set the club earlier into a lighter position, making it easier to control the weight of the club.

5

The Arc
Player

Body type: ectomorph

Distinguishing feature: the "long" spine

Dominant dimension: height

Dominant power source: swing arc

Swing motion: figure-8 inside drop

Overall look: slinging

Finish position: Back bow (reverse C)

Shaft load profile: no bursts

(TOP LEFT) *The right foot is in a square position, and the left foot is flared. The shoulders and two arms form a triangle.*

(TOP RIGHT) *The takeaway begins with the shoulders and arms extending the club down the line and the right hip turning back off the line.*

(BOTTOM) *The weight has remained on the inside of the right foot. The right arm still has not folded, so the hands and the club head are the same height—and he's halfway to the top. That's the way Jack Nicklaus looked in his prime.*

Just before the club reaches the top of the backswing, the weight begins to transfer to the left hip, creating the left-side pivot point — and it happens before the club has even reached the top of the swing. With these high hands, the hips will have to move laterally during the downswing to wait for the hands.

The hips have waited, and the hands and the club have been dropped down in front of the body with plenty of space to work with. The left hip is beginning to turn out of the way, and the left wall is forming.

(TOP LEFT) *The left hip has fully cleared, the left leg has straightened, and the club head is released into the back of the ball.*

(TOP RIGHT) *Both arms are fully extended as the club has been released over the left wall.*

(BOTTOM) *He has finished in a classic reverse C position with the body fully turned through and the hands and arms in a high, extended position.*

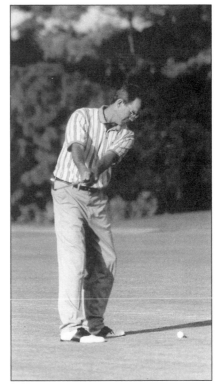

The arc player's posture is in an erect position, so his chest allows forty-five degrees of arm swing, a criterion for his one-piece take-away. The heels are closed to encourage the hip bump that starts the downswing. The bump—where the hips move along the heel line—gives the hands time to get into hitting position. And it's all set up at address. Maybe that's why they call it the setup.

The chest is the master mover in the arc swing, so the shoulders, arms, hands, and club move as a unit. The club and the arms are extending over the ball of the foot line. The key here is the straight right arm, which insures that this club is on its way up (the height dimension), not around (the depth dimension).

(OPPOSITE TOP LEFT) Because of the right leg post, the weight is on the inner rim of the right foot as the right arm folds to elevate the club into the height dimension. Everything necessary for the arc swing— foot position, grip, posture, and so on—is designed to drive the club away and then up.

(TOP RIGHT) *At the top of the back-swing, the right leg has fully posted, setting up the downswing fall to the left. The left arm is above the shoulder plane, creating a very upright swing plane. The hands are high and are the slowest hands in that they must travel the farthest of all three swing types to get back to impact. The slightly open face will cause a handsy-looking release.*

(BOTTOM) *Here the club head enters the depth dimension, and it is the reason that it looks like the club has looped as it returns to the shaft plane. The weight has shifted from his right heel, cross laterally, to the ball of his left foot. His arms have dropped the club back onto the shaft-plane angle.*

(TOP RIGHT) *His hips have rotated throughout to impact as he slings the club out from under his neck. He's strong, and he can keep his upper spine from sliding forward, a move that leads to the reverse C finish.*

(TOP LEFT) *Both arms are extended in a full release because the club head has swung out from under him rather than around him. His right heel is up but still looking at the ground, showing the flexibility of the prototype arc player.*

(BOTTOM) *He has finished with high hands and in perfect balance. Looking at this sequence, it's obvious that you must be strong and flexible to be an arc player and that if you are, the power can be awesome.*

As an arc player, you have a long swing with a lot of lower-body action, and when your timing is off, you can hit some wild shots. But when your timing is good, you can bring a golf course to its knees because you are very long and accurate. Yours is a high-maintenance swing that requires a lot of practice. Because of the reverse C finish, it also requires a lot of flexibility, and this is the reason the arc swing is often labeled the bad-back swing.

As powerful as it is, the arc swing can get off track because you have long arms, a thin chest, and considerable flexibility, so it's easy to swing the club too far around and behind you. This traps the club and prevents you from returning it in front of your body in time for impact. Thus, the depth dimension (the "around") is the arc player's nemesis. To avoid this, the arc player must employ a one-piece take-away in which the upper body turns first, raising the arms. The late weight shift delays the hip turn long enough for the arms to swing up. This move is seen most clearly in the swings of Colin Montgomery and Phil Michelson. The arc downswing is characterized by a shift-then-turn action in which the weight moves to the left side even before the backswing is completed.

One advantage of the arc swing is that as you get older and lose flexibility, your swing becomes shorter and more controlled. Johnny Miller said that when John Daly is ninety years old, his incredibly long backswing swing should shorten to just about parallel.

Good models for you as an arc player are Payne Stewart, Fred Couples, Don January, Johnny Miller, Phil Michelson, Scott Hoch, Lee Janzen, Paul Stankowski, Davis Love, Michelle McGann, and Betsy King.

The Building Blocks for the Arc Player

TASK 1: THE SETUP

As with all swing types, the preparation stage for an arc player has five parts, beginning with the grip.

The face of the club points to the target line. Note the retracted (short) thumb.

Left Hand Grip: Neutral to Strongish. Holding the club in your left hand, trap the handle under the fat pad of your left hand, with your left thumb just to the right side of the shaft. Position the club shaft diagonally to the target line with the head of the club resting directly in front of your right toe on the toe line. This helps the handle to fit across your left palm with your thumb retracted on the handle, a configuration we call "the short thumb." The retracted short-thumb position promotes a later setting of your wrists. This procedure matches the erect posture that helps restrict the excess arm swing common to arc-swing body types. Your left-hand grip ranges from strong, like Fred Couples's, to more neutral, like Davis Love's.

Right Hand Grip: Neutral. Once your left hand is in position, lift the club chest-high, and place the fingers of your right hand around the handle so the knuckles of both hands form a continuous line. This puts your right hand more on top of the handle in a neutral position, neither weak nor strong, and encourages a straight right arm during the takeaway, directing your club upward and protecting it from the depth dimension on the way back.

Ball Position. Since your hips move laterally toward the target in the downswing, you'll need more time to get to the ball, so you should play the ball farther forward than other swing types. This forward

The neutral grip of the arc player makes the release look handsy.

ball position also gives your shoulders time to turn back to the ball and square the club face at impact.

The arc player should use the following three ball positions: for the mid to short irons, position the ball in the middle of the left half of your chest, off the logo of your shirt; for long irons and fairway woods position the ball in line with your left underarm, opposite your left heel; for the driver and other woods off a tee, play the ball off the tip of your left shoulder. As the ball moves forward in your stance with the driver, it must also be positioned *along the path* or curve of the swing rather than the target line. If you just move the ball forward along the target line, by the time your club head reaches the ball, it will be moving inside the line, and you'll hit the ball on

The arc swing entails the most forward ball positions of the three swing types because of the lateral hip movement.

the toe of the club. Therefore, when you position the ball forward when teeing with a wood, remember to move the ball *closer* to you.

Posture. Good posture puts you in a balanced, ready-for-action position. Posture also dictates the plane angle of your golf swing as well as the amount your arms swing before your left arm runs into your chest. As we've said before, your thin chest makes it's easy to swing your arms too far behind you. As an arc player, you should stand with moderate knee flex, depending on your build. Your tailbone should be out and up as though you were about to sit on a high bar stool. This gives you the proper counterbalance to the tilt of your upper body. Please note that arc players should not squat at address.

Pinch your knees in toward each other in a slightly knock-kneed position, and favor your right foot with more than 50 percent of your weight: for the irons, 40 percent left/60 percent right; for the woods, 25/75. This is the arc preloading position, and it keeps weight on the inner rim of your right foot throughout your backswing, a necessity for establishing your right side as a buttress against which to turn. Preloading also encourages the left knee to move behind the ball, lowering your left side and setting up the fall to the left during your downswing.

Stance: The Flare to Square. The stance is the foundation for your preparation stage. It determines the distance your lower body will move laterally in your downswing, as well as the timing and direction of your weight transfer.

Begin by setting your right foot perpendicular to the target line. This position "posts" the right leg, causing it to straighten but not lock in the backswing. At the same time your right hip will rise slightly, setting up the diagonal hip bump in the downswing. If you're like most golfers, you judge foot position by the position of your big toe, but this can be deceptive. Because of the curve of the human foot, what looks to be perpendicular to the target line, as judged by the toes, is actually flared open. Turning the right toe slightly inward at address is the correct way to arrive at a truly square position in which a line drawn from the outside edge of your foot is perpendicular to the target line.

With the right foot truly perpendicular, it appears to be toed in.

How you arrange your feet at address influences two of the most important aspects of your swing: your coil and your release. It's not turning that maximizes power, it's coil. Coil means turning the top of your body more than the lower to generate springlike power. By doing this efficiently, you maximize your distance with all your clubs.

But if your right side gives way to the pressure exerted on it in the backswing, very little coil is produced. To create coil, your right foot and leg must act as stabilizers, providing resistance as your upper body turns into or against your lower right side. One way to create resistance is by setting your right foot perpendicular to the target line, using the proper part of your foot as you align. Anatomically, the outside of your right foot is curved from the ball of your foot to your toes and straight from the ball of your foot back to your heel. The problem is that since almost all arc players use their toes as the guide to position their feet, they unintention-ally flare their right foot at address, weakening the right side and decreasing its ability to provide resistance.

103

To make sure your right foot is pointing where you want it to, use the straight part of your foot for alignment. If you're supple, with a high-swing speed, your foot should be perpendicular to your intended line of flight to provide the maximum brace. If your flexibility is moderate to low, you need a longer swing arc; close your stance and flare out your right foot to allow a bigger turn.

Once you've placed your right foot perpendicular to the target line, position your left foot in a slightly closed position. Then flare your left foot until the line of your toes is square to the target line. In the LAWs model this is termed "flare to square," and it creates a condition in which your toe line is parallel with the target line but your heels are slightly closed. Since your hips will follow your heel line, flare to square sets up the lateral hip bump in your downswing.

Left-Foot Flare. The amount you flare your left foot has a direct effect on the slotting of the club and the timing of your release of the club head to the ball. This is because the release of the angle between your left forearm and your club shaft is a result of your left side straightening through impact. In so doing you create resistance (the left-side wall) and cause your hands to sling the club head through the ball. The more your left foot flares, the later you establish your left-side wall, and, therefore, the later the club head is released. Conversely, the more perpendicular your left foot is to the target line, the earlier the release will be.

Stance Width. As you'll see in chapter 6, the width of your stance has much to do with the amount of lateral motion in your swing: the wider your stance is, the more your hips move laterally, and the narrower your stance, the more your hips will rotate. Since arc players swing the club in a high arc, a lot of lateral motion is needed to give the club time to get down to the ball from its position high above you.

Your stance width is determined in part by the length of your arms. Once again we see the influence that the time dimension has on a golf swing, because the longer the arms, the higher your swing arc. For this reason you need more time for your club to get back in front of your body at impact. Lateral hip motion gives you this time, the amount of which is governed by the width of your stance. Long arms match with a wider stance, while short arms match with a narrow stance. Note that "long" and "short" are relative to the rest of your body. If you're six feet tall with thirty-inch arms, you're a short-armed arc player, and your stance will look narrow for your height. If you're five-foot-nine with thirty-two-inch arms, your stance would be wider than normal.

As a starting point, normal is defined in terms of a range of foot widths that depend on the club you're using—the longer the club, the wider the stance. For a full swing with a short iron, the narrowest that the stance should be is hip-width, measured from the outside of the hips. For the driver, the narrowest your stance should be is shoulder-width, measured at the tips of the shoulders.

You should experiment to find your perfect stance width, but a good way to begin is as follows: form a pistol with your right hand as it hangs at your side. Fold your arm up as far as it will go, keeping your elbow in place against your side. Now measure the distance between your thumb and the top of your shoulder. Use this distance to establish how much wider than normal you should make your stance. If the distance is two inches, for example, then your stance should be two inches wider than hip-width for the shortest clubs and two inches wider than shoulder-width for the longest clubs.

Aim/Alignment. First aim your club face at the target; then, as an arc player, position your shoulders and feet parallel to the target line. But because your heels are slightly closed (your heel line, if extended, would intersect the target line at some point in front of the ball), take care to close your hips by the same amount that your heels are closed. Your hips and heels should therefore be slightly closed, while your shoulders, toe line, and club face should be square.

TASK 2: TAKEAWAY

Think of your takeaway in terms of a boulder teetering at the top of a mountain. With just the touch of a finger you could send the boulder tumbling over the edge, but once it's set in motion, it's out of your control. The same is true of your takeaway. At the start of your swing, everything must move slowly and in harmony to set the club on the proper path and keep it under control. Manipulating or jerking the club away from the ball in this sensitive period can set the arc player on a course for disaster.

A good one-piece takeaway, like Payne Stewart's, looks peaceful because everything moves together. In a one-piece takeaway, everything in your upper body, including the club, moves away from the ball in harmony. In the golf swing some movements are sequential while others are simultaneous; the arc player's takeaway is a perfect example of a simultaneous movement in which your club, hands, arms, shoulders, and chest start away from the ball as a unit. At waist high the toe of your club face should be tilted slightly forward toward the target line, matching your spine angle; your hands and the club head are the same height.

Your right arm should stay straight until you can't extend the club any farther, and the back of your right hand should point at an angle to the sky. Your right hand will begin to rotate as soon as your right elbow folds, and by the time you arrive at the top of your swing, the club face will be square or slightly open.

The Chest Is the Master Mover

Arc swings like Davis Love's and Payne Stewart's look so smooth because their perfectly synchronized turning motion is keyed by the upper body. When the chest turns, your arms, hands, and club move with it naturally unless you do something to prevent it. This graceful, fluid motion is what makes the classic arc swing so beautiful to observe. As an arc player, you should feel as though your chest is the master mover of the club. You need to forget about trying to swing the club head, the club handle, your arms, or your hands; that's simply bad advice for a person of your body type.

TASK 3: THE LOADING ZONE

The loading zone is the area between the end of your takeaway and the top of your swing, where your power load takes place. Since you have an extended, one-piece takeaway with a preload at address, you shift your weight later than other swing types, and it happens in conjunction with the setting of your wrists and the folding of your right elbow.

Your takeaway is dedicated to creating width, and once that is done, you achieve height, as you continue your shoulder turn, by folding your right elbow and cocking your wrists, a movement that puts your arms in a very high position, with your left thumb underneath the shaft for support.

In the height dimension, your club head is packed with the power of potential energy. Your high-handed position not only stores potential energy for power, but it also sets up the fall to the left during the downswing, a move that is so noticeable in a classic arc swing like that of Fred Couples.

At the top of the backswing, your left knee has moved behind the ball, lowering your left hip a touch. Neither your knees nor your hips are level, but your left heel is raised. Your right forearm is straight up and down, a configuration that, for the more flexible arc player, causes the club shaft to cross the line and point to the right of the target. If done correctly, with coil, crossing the line is a positive action that increases the distance (arc) that the club head travels.

Note that your flexibility is an asset only when it is used correctly to access your power source—the height and length of your swing arc.

The Long Spine

A distinguishing feature of an arc player is the creation of the long spine at the top of the swing and at impact. During the backswing your hips tilt so that the right hip is over the right heel and your right leg is straight but not completely locked, giving the appear-

This is a visual representation of the spine lining up with the left hip and leg at impact.

ance that your lower spine is in line with your right hip and creating a direct line from the top of the spine to the ankle. Your weight is on the inside rim of your right foot. This posting of the right side is the reason great players like the young Johnny Miller and Jack Nicklaus looked as if they'd left too much weight on their left side. But don't be fooled. The majority of weight is in the right hip, and they're using the right side as a post.

TASK 4: SLOTTING THE CLUB IN THE DOWNSWING

The downswing starts with a shift of your weight to the left hip and then a turn to the ball once your arms have dropped into position.

As you swing the club up and over your body, it's momentum that triggers the downswing by moving the weight into the left hip. Once this has taken place, the hip bump occurs—a lateral shuttle of your hips toward the target. To maintain balance coming back to the ball, your weight must switch from the heel of the right foot to the ball of your left foot. This cross-lateral weight shift at the start of the down-swing keeps your hips and shoulders a bit closed—just long enough for the club to drop into the slot. Now the club is in position for the powerful scissors leg action, so characteristic of all long hitters, in which the right leg and hip hit across a firm left leg.

The Long Left Spine. It's the hip bump that gives your club time to drop onto a shallow approach trajectory. If your hips turn before the bump, the club is pushed out toward the target line, creating a cut-across club-head path. The central pivot point of your upper body—your swing center—is located just below your throat and must hold its position while your head drops back and downward in response

Kermit Zarley establishes the left wall.

to the force of your swing. With your hips moving laterally and your swing center staying in place, the long left spine is created, a position that leads to the reverse C, a bowing of the back during your follow-through.

TASK 5: DELIVERY ZONE

Immediately after your weight moves to the ball of your left foot, your hips begin turning behind you, which moves the club head from inside to out toward the ball. While you're actually using a combination of body, hand, and arm release, the appearance is one of a slashing, handsy swing.

Your club head squares to the ball because your lower left leg stands firm as your upper leg and hip continue to pull up and away

Because he stayed behind the ball through impact, Zarley finishes in the reverse C.

from it. The collision between the rotating right side and the firm left side causes the release of your club head; because your right leg and hip have fired across your left (the same scissoring action that a home-run hitter uses), your club head is swung at great speeds through the hitting zone.

TASK 6: THE FINISH

The high acceleration of your club head as it slams into the ball causes the body to rebound into the characteristic arc follow-through. Since you have a fixed axis at the top of the spine, your lower body actually swings out from under your neck, creating the reverse C finish position so characteristic of the arc swing. Your arms are in a high position over your left shoulder, your chest is facing the target, and your body is bowed, with your head over your right foot.

Arc Summary

During the backswing your club moves away, up and over your body at the top of your swing, and out from under it through impact. In the arc swing everything from your stance to your hip bump is geared to operating in the height dimension.

As you swing away from the ball, your lower spine shifts in line with your right leg and hip; then, during the downswing, it shifts in line with your left hip and leg. This creation of the long spine is the hallmark of the arc swing. There is, however, no floating of the upper spine, and since the top of your spine is fixed, your shoulder turn is much steeper than the other swing types. Also, because the top of your spine is fixed, the club slings out from under you as it runs into the left-side wall, causing a body recoil that ends in the reverse C position.

ARC POWER LEAKS

Takeaway. As an arc player your dominant power source is the length and height of your swing arc. You generate power by swinging your club high above you, but you must take care to do it with coil and not to lift the club to the top of your swing using only your arms and hands. Remember—*if you go back lifting, you come down chopping,* and that spells power leak.

The problem is that if you break up your one-piece takeaway, which piece do you move first? Sometimes you'll start with your front shoulder, or maybe your hands or left knee. This is why you've got to commit yourself to the one-piece concept with your chest as the master mover that initiates all motion so that your shoulders, arms, hands, and club move together as a unit.

Right-Foot Flare. When you flare your back foot at address, your one-piece takeaway turns the club directly behind you on much too flat an arc. From here you have no choice but to come over the top as you start back to the ball, a weak and indirect route to impact. Since you want to swing the club up rather than around you, position your right foot perpendicular to the target line with no flare at all. This will plug your power leak by forcing both your right side and your club to ride upward into your dominant power zone, the height dimension.

Backswing Tilting. Knowing that you need to swing the club in a high arc above you, it's easy to make the mistake of tilting the triangle—formed by the chest, arms, and shoulders—down toward the ground during your backswing. Tilting pulls the top of the spine down and forward, thereby destroying the central axis of the arc swing. Since the top of the spine is the fixed axis of the arc swing, it must stay put during your backswing.

Downswing: Fixed Spine. As we outlined above, the key to power in your arc swing is to keep the top of your spine fixed so your downswing unfolds around it. You start the downswing with a pronounced lateral hip move that keeps your hips pointing to the right of the target. This slightly closed hip position creates space for your arms to slot the club to the inside. Once this happens, your hips snap open, swinging the club head into the ball with tremendous velocity.

This tilt robs him of power.

At these speeds any movement of the top of the spine forward is a power robber of major proportions.

Elbow Fold. Allowing your right elbow to fold and pull backward during the takeaway is a major power leak. When this happens, the club head is dragged to the inside, and that which goes inward must also go up steeply and then out toward the ball to start the down-swing. Thus, you've committed an over-the-top move, a major error for the arc player. Folding your elbow too early also produces a lift-ing motion that creates a narrow arc, just the opposite of what an arc

113

Sliding ahead of the ball causes a melting of the left wall; note how the left knee has collapsed.

player wants. Your right arm will fold correctly if your one-piece takeaway is correct. Our advice is to let your right arm fold in response to the swinging motion of your triangle.

There are some arc players such as Fred Couples who fold the right elbow earlier than the prototype suggests, but they do not allow the elbow to pull backward. Folding the elbow elevates the club head, but pulling the elbow inward deepens the club head. The former (folding) gives height; the latter (pulling) buries the club head in the depth dimension, unplugging the arc player from his dominant power source.

Arc Swing Adjustments

As we have said, the arc player is usually thin-chested, long-limbed, and very flexible. When arc players are missing one of these characteristics, their setup must be adjusted so that their swing can work for them, not against them.

An arc player with a thick chest will require a more bent-over posture to create more room for the proper arm swing. An arc player with a long torso and short legs will require a swing that has less lateral motion with the hips than the model suggests. The swing will not be as upright, and to facilitate this posture, the left knee will be pinched in more at address, to encourage it to point behind the ball at the top of the backswing. The left-hand grip will be stronger with a narrower stance to help the swing become more rotary. The right hand will be slightly stronger, allowing the right arm to fold earlier to help flatten the swing plane.

An arc player with a short torso and long legs will have a lot of lateral motion in the hips; this movement will be facilitated by pointing the left knee in the direction of the flared left foot. The stance will be wider to encourage lateral motion. The right-hand grip will be weaker (more on top) to create a more upright swing that meshes with the lateral hip motion. There should also be a more erect posture to create a more level shoulder turn.

An arc player with longer arms requires a wider stance (about an inch wider than normal for every inch by which their wingspan exceeds their height) to create more lateral hip motion to slot the club on the downswing. The posture will also be more erect to reduce arm swing and preserve the one-piece takeaway.

An arc player with shorter arms will have a stronger right-hand grip to allow the right arm to fold earlier and a stronger left-hand grip to match the motion of the hips. He will also have a narrower stance, making the lower body more rotary and less lateral. The ball position is more centered than the prototype suggests, to match both the grip and the lower-body action.

115

ADJUSTMENTS FOR THE OLDER ARC PLAYER (ARC-IVER)

With age-induced loss of flexibility, the arc swing moves toward the width dimension, prompting three adjustments.

1. The right foot is dropped back to increase the turn and create width during the takeaway. The foot is still square, and thus the right side still straightens.
2. The ball position is moved back in the stance with a stronger grip to accommodate a lower hand position at the top.
3. The posture is more bent over, allowing a fluid arm swing and complementing the stronger grip.
4. The stance is narrower to minimize the lateral motion matching the shorter swing.

For the less flexible senior, the right foot is flared to allow for more turn.

THE JUNIOR ARC PLAYER (NEW ARCER)

For younger arc players the stance is square or even a bit open to restrict flexibility and turn. The grip is stronger to help square the club face and create an earlier and lighter set of the club. The ball position is in more of a standard leverage position to coincide with the grip.

THE WOMAN ARC PLAYER (JOAN OF ARC)

Due to lack of strength, the right arm should fold earlier to help work the club into a lighter, more vertical position. The left hand can also be strengthened to offset the opening of the club face.

6

The Width Player

Body type: endomorph

Distinguishing feature: spinal float

Dominant dimension: width

Dominant power source: physical strength

Swing motion: pushing

Overall look: "punch motion"

Shaft load profile: one burst

Finish position: no bow (I position)

The model for the face-on swing sequence is a very powerful, muscular-advantage player with a large chest and minimal flexibility —an MA1.

117

(TOP LEFT) *The width player has a slightly wider than shoulder width stance. His ball position is in the center of his body with both feet flared to increase his ability to turn.*

(TOP RIGHT) *The backswing begins with the left shoulder turning behind the ball. If you match his head position in frames I and II to the space in the tree in the background, you can see the beginning of the head float, a key to the width swing.*

(BOTTOM) *The club is set into a wide position, with the left hand pushing down on the handle and the right hand pushing the club away.*

At the top of the backswing, the left shoulder is almost over the right foot, and the club is fully set in the width dimension. The shaft and shoulders are perpendicular to each other in a three-quarters position. Here the head float, part of the moving coil of the width player, is apparent.

Here the right elbow tucks into the right side, shallowing out the swing by bringing the shaft back onto the swing-plane angle. Meanwhile, the body, including the head, is moving laterally back to its address position.

(OPPOSITE TOP LEFT) *Once the slotting is completed, the width player turns his left hip out of the way to hit the ball. At impact his lower body is a solid platform from which to hit. Note that the swing center located just below the throat is back to where it started, insuring that one stays behind the ball through impact.*

(TOP RIGHT) *He has released his right side, holding nothing back. As he rotates on his left hip, his back foot is a rudder for balance.*

(BOTTOM) *He finishes in the classic straight up-and-down I position, with all his weight on the left side.*

Given his flexibility level, this is the only way he can make a good swing and take advantage of his upper-body strength without losing his balance. If he had never played before and you put him on a desert island with unlimited range balls, this is the swing you'd see upon returning two years later.

*The model for the down-the-line se-
quence is a smaller-chested MA2, a
strong player with a bit more flexibility than the MA1; his swing reflects it,
showing less lateral movement.*

*His stance is slightly closed to
allow him to him make a bigger
turn, a match for his lack of flexibility. His posture is bent over more
from the hip, a match for his large
chest, which creates room for his
arms to swing.*

*Not a hint here of picking the club
up. The hands and the club head are
at the same height as the left shoulder turns behind the ball, extending
both of his arms into the width
dimension.*

(OPPOSITE TOP LEFT) *Both hands
have fully set the club into a steep
position in front of his chest with his
left arm on the toe line. Because of
the closed stance, he's in the depth
dimension but still able to keep the
club wide and away from him.
Because he has low hands, and a
high club head, the shaft is vertical
at this point. The club head is high
without the player having to exceed
his level of flexibility.*

(TOP RIGHT) *At the top of his three-quarters backswing, his upper body has moved behind the ball, loading his right side for a powerful downswing. His hands are centered in the middle of his chest, a position that makes the width player's hands the fastest of the three swing types.*

(BOTTOM) *The simultaneous move of the left hip beginning to turn back over the left heel and the right elbow tucking into the side begins the downswing. Compare the club shaft in the last three frames where it goes from upright to just right— it's the tuck that shallows the club back onto the swing-plane angle, in preparation for the hit delivered by the upper body.*

(TOP LEFT) *At impact his hips have cleared with the right heel down and slightly angled to the inside. The swing must be repetitive, which is why the lower body is used as a rock-solid platform from which to hit through impact. No "Elvis legs" here.*

(TOP RIGHT) *The shoulders have continued to turn through, extending both the arms and the club down the line.*

(BOTTOM) *He finishes in a balanced I position, the club around his body and his belt buckle facing the target.*

There are two body types that favor a width swing:

- **Width 1:** A thick-chested person with a rounded shape with short arms and legs. This person is physically strong and often has limited flexibility (referred to in the LAWs model as the muscular-advantage golfer). There are two subtypes of the muscular-advantage player, MA1 and MA2. MA1 has a very large chest and short arms like Craig Stadler, Duffy Waldorf, and Craig Parry. MA2 has a medium-large chest and normal to long arms, as do Tom Lehman and Peter Jacobsen.

- **Width 2:** Golfers with very limited flexibility. They have a range of strength levels but are usually on the weak side. They can exhibit a variety of body shapes and contours, but usually their body has markedly diminished strength and flexibility because of aging. If you're a W2 who is not very strong and who has minimal flexibility, you don't have the option to swing the club up and over, as an arc player does. Your shape and flexibility level make this physically impossible. And you can't swing the club around your body without forcing yourself out of your golf posture. Thus, by a process of elimination, you need to swing the club away from your body, establishing width as your dominant power source (DPS). Many older players and large-chested, nonmuscular females fall into this category.

Why the Width Dimension?

A broadly built person usually has difficulty getting sufficient arm swing because he is blocked by his thick chest. Minimal flexibility makes it difficult to swing around the body without straightening up. Players with large chests have even greater problems trying to swing the club high above them without tilting toward the target at the top of the swing. So, like the W2 described above, a W1 needs to swing the club away from the body in the width dimension.

The king, Arnold Palmer, is an MA2 who can still give it a ride.

The prototypical width player relies on a strong upper body to hit the ball. Craig Stadler, Bruce Lietzke, Arnold Palmer, Hal Sutton, Rocco Mediate, Tom Wargo, Jim Albus, Peter Jacobsen, Duffy Waldorf, and Laura Davis are excellent examples of width players who exploit the strength and mass of their upper body. They are truly muscularly advantaged and are more hitters than swingers, a characteristic that becomes evident at impact, when they smash the ball using the large muscles of the upper body. The width swing with a large chest employs a turn-then-shift action to start the downswing, when the first move is a repositioning of the club by turning the shoulders, giving the appearance of an early over-the-top move. Once the club is slotted, the weight shift occurs. For smaller-chested players this preslotting of the club before the weight shift does not occur. Thus for both builds you should swing the club away from your body, establishing width as your dominant dimension.

Two Types of Width Players

The width player on the left (a former tour player and an MA1) has a larger chest and less flexibility than the one on the right (MA2).

The two types of MA players take different paths to the ball, depending on the size of the chest. MA1 players with very large chests have more of a vertical shaft on the backswing and come over the top of their toe line but back onto the target line. Examples are the swings of David Ogrin, Bruce Lietzke, and Mark McCumber. Those who swing this way primarily fade the ball.

For the smaller-chested (MA2) player with more flexibility, the club travels on a shallower swing plane, approaching the ball from inside the toe line and releasing the club head onto the target. Tom Wargo, Arnold Palmer, and John Cook exemplify this approach.

Tom Wargo has tucked his elbow, a move that will bring the club down on a very direct route to the ball.

TASK 1: SETUP

Our advice is to use the model as a starting point, following it to the letter. From there you'll customize your swing by experimenting with variations of the width swing that work for you.

Grip. With your right hand hold the club in front of you with the shaft aligned vertically to the ground. Place the club across the base of the fingers of your left hand, and extend your left thumb flush with the handle. This long thumb lets your wrists set more readily, giving the club head the added height it needs. Now close the fingers of your left hand around the grip, and place your left palm closer to the top of the handle in a strong grip position, similar to the way you would hold a hammer.

Here is the fully extended long thumb of the width player that helps him to cock his wrists.

To facilitate the wrist set and extension during the takeaway, place your right hand in a slightly weaker-than-standard position, with the V pointing toward your nose. In many cases width players have large, inflexible wrists that roll more easily than they cock, and this combination of strong left hand and weak right hand allows the push-set cocking action you need for your width takeaway.

You should hold the grip in the fingers of both hands, which makes it easy to set the club aggressively without swinging your arms high above you. This grip also discourages you from trying to turn your arms and the club around your body, a fatal move for a width player. And please don't be afraid to try the baseball grip, with all ten fingers on the handle. If you have very thick, inflexible wrists, the baseball grip can help you set the club more easily.

Ball Position. Since the width swing calls for a closed body alignment and a strong left-hand grip, the lowest point of your swing arc occurs early; therefore, the ball must be farther back in your stance than in the other swing types. Be careful to adjust your body for the correct ball position, because when the ball is farther back in your stance, the tendency is to aim to the right of the target.

For short and medium irons, position the ball in the center of your stance, opposite your nose. Playing the ball a bit farther back than standard accommodates your strong left-hand grip, flattish shoulder turn, and closed body alignment. With long irons and fairway woods move the ball slightly forward of center about a ball width, opposite your left cheek. For your driver and other woods off a tee, position the ball opposite the center of the left side of your chest, where the

The neutral right hand allows the club to be set correctly in the width dimension.

logo on your shirt would be. The more flexible you are and the smaller your chest, the less you should close your stance. This means that your ball position will move farther forward than the prototype suggests.

Stance and Foot Flare. To accommodate your build, make the following adjustments: first, flare your feet to maximize your ability to turn back and through the ball. Because of the combination of limited flexibility and a large chest, you have difficulty turning into the depth dimension from a square stance. This is why you draw your back foot away from the toe line, closing your stance. Remember that your knees always go in the direction of your feet, so flaring allows you to turn your hip over your heel without straightening your right leg. It also helps you keep your right heel from flipping

Of the three types, the width player positions the ball the farthest back in the stance.

up and out toward the target line in the downswing, a move that forces your right hip to spin toward the target.

Your left foot should also flare out just the right amount: too much flare will result in a late club release; too little will cause you to release your angles of power prematurely.

With a little experimentation, it's simple to find how much flare you need. Take a square stance, placing a shaft on the ground from your right heel to left toe and one from your left heel to right toe. The shafts will both form 45° angles off the target line. Now place a shaft across the tops of your thighs, and turn your right hip back over the right heel. Find the amount of flare in your right foot that allows you to complete your backswing without straightening your right leg. Now flare your left foot, and make several mock swings turning your left hip until the shaft on your thighs and the shaft on the ground match up at impact and your left leg straightens. This means that your hips reach the correct impact position at the same time your left leg formed the left wall, insuring a burst of power at exactly the right point.

Stance Width. To find how much to close your stance and to gauge the stance width that allows you to bend from your hips and still remain in balance, do the following: set up with your feet parallel to the target line. Now swing to the top, and in slow motion, turn through into your finish position, and notice the gap between your knees. Then simply slide your back foot back until your knees come together (see photos on page 133).

Aim/Alignment. Basically, you aim the club face and then align your body; a lot of confusion and swing errors occur if you don't keep the two separate. When you're aiming the club face, "open" means it points to the right of the target, "closed" to the left. But when you're aligning your body lines (shoulders, hips, knees, and feet), open means pointed to the left and closed to the right. This point of confusion comes about because in a square position, your body line is parallel to the target line, while your club face is perpendicular to it. The important point here is not to confuse the two and always to *aim your club face before aligning your body.* You might be able to get

Finding the correct flare provides a solid left wall at impact. He knows his flare is correct when the shaft across his thighs and the one on the ground match.

away with a misaligned body for awhile, but an improperly aimed club face is a guarantee of trouble.

As a muscular-advantage player, you want to aim both your club face and your body at the target so that your body line is slightly closed. Aim your club face at the target, and take a square stance. Then, without changing your square club face, drop your right foot back away from the target line, and allow your hips and shoulders to follow.

If you're a width player by default (W2—you don't have a large chest, but you lack strength and flexibility), you'll also modify your aim and alignment as the MA player does by closing your feet and hips so they point at the target. This gives you more freedom to turn. Your shoulders, however, should stay in a standard position, parallel to the target.

This player is finding out how much to close his stance. He takes his position and then turns through to impact.

To find how much he needs to close his stance, he slides his back knee until it just touches his left.

Posture. As a width player, your posture serves an important role in allowing you sufficient arm swing. By increasing the amount you bend from the hips, your arms will swing more freely across your chest.

First, take a standard address position by bending from the hips and adding some knee flex. Let your arms hang straight down. Now swing your left arm across your chest. If it goes more than forty-five degrees before its stopped, you're bent over too far; if it can't reach the forty-five-degree mark, then you're too upright. Simply adjust the amount of bend until your left arm can swing about forty-five degrees across your chest.

The bottom line is this: the larger your chest, the more you'll bend from the hips. We call it *buying the correct amount of arm swing with your posture,* a key concept in the LAWs model for all swing types.

Please remember to make the following adjustments: if your posture is more upright, your stance is less closed; the more you bend from the hips, the more you draw your right foot back. By making these adjustments, you'll have the most direct route to the ball.

A suggestion: as part of your preshot routine, take special care to position your left arm directly on top of your chest rather than beside it. Too many width players ruin their posture and thus their swing by allowing their left arm to hang at the side of the chest at address, thereby blocking the correct takeaway.

The Backswing. Your backswing is divided into two parts, the takeaway and the loading zone.

TASK 2: THE TAKEAWAY

The takeaway begins with the left shoulder turning behind the ball. When the hands reach a point above the right knee, the heel pad of your left hand pushes down on the club handle to cock your wrists. This motion sets the club shaft on a slightly more upright angle than is standard, just above your right shoulder. Since you've now created the space a width player needs between his body and his hands, you have room to drop the club onto the correct plane in the downswing. This happens when your right elbow tucks as it returns to your right side during the downswing.

In conjunction with your left hand action, your right hand pushes down on the knuckle of your left thumb to extend your arms away from your body. This movement is another way to create the necessary width — it forces the butt of the club down and away from the chest.

You set your wrists as your arms swing away from the ball. This setting action pushes the club away from your body, with the right palm operating like a stiff-arm in football.

TASK 3: LOADING ZONE

The push-set wrist action increases the gap between your hands and chest in the width dimension. It is the key to your swing because it gives your club head height but leaves your hands low and wide, which is a more comfortable and appropriate position for your body type. It also equips you with leverage that multiplies club-head speed because of the power angle established between your left forearm and the club shaft.

Simply turn your upper body level around your inclined spine until your left shoulder is behind the ball. If you are flexible enough, the shoulder should go over the right knee. Keep your left heel flat on the ground to build coil as your upper body turns against your lower body. This will shorten your swing but preserve its width and coil, i.e., power.

You should feel as though your backswing is complete when your left arm is parallel to the ground, although momentum will take your swing a bit farther, to about a three-quarters position. But at the top of your backswing, your club should be short of parallel with your arms, extended away from your body and your hands in front of your chest.

Head Float. During your takeaway your right elbow stays straight until it bends to elevate the club. The amount and timing of this elevation once again depends on the size of your chest. But if your setup and takeaway are correct, it will happen automatically. It is similar to the arc takeaway except that your upper spine floats behind the ball as your backswing coil develops. Thus your chest turns away from the target, taking everything in the upper body with it, including your head. Note that the head doesn't flop from side to side during your swing—it simply stays positioned in the middle of your shoulders as you turn back and through.

We call the head/spine float the *moving coil*, and it is the hallmark of the width swing. When we teach the moving coil to students, invariably they say it feels like a sway, but it isn't. A sway occurs when your right hip moves laterally outside your right heel, whereas in the moving coil the spine and head float back as your weight moves to your right hip, not outside it. This is a necessary accommodation to a body type not suited to twisting itself up like a pretzel. If you anchor your spine and head during your backswing, you'll have no extension and minimum coil. If you try to swing the club with a fixed spine, your left shoulder will never turn behind the ball, your left arm runs into the chest too early and, to continue the swing, something has to give — you would either have to take the club outside or lift it off plane.

Top of the Swing. Be careful not to let your right arm dominate your backswing — it will cause your swing to go too high above your shoulders. When that happens, your left arm must follow, and that results in a slice. Since your left arm has a greater distance to travel and you're not a flexible person, this forces you out of your golf posture and ruins your swing.

To find the position that best fits your flexibility, use the following technique, which is outlined in chapter 3. Without a club, take your address position and, using only your right arm, simulate a full backswing. Stop at the top and bring your left hand up to meet your right hand. If you can do this while keeping your golf posture intact, you know where your backswing should end. But if there is a gap between the two, your right arm has swung too far. Correct this by bringing your right hand down to meet your left: this is your perfect top-of-the-swing position.

If you have some special characteristics — right-shoulder problems, a very large chest, or an inability to rotate your right forearm so that it's perpendicular with the ground — then your backswing will be steeper than normal. In this case your right forearm naturally flies, as does Jack Nicklaus's, and it tilts toward the target line as your right elbow folds. This sets your shaft upright to the sky, much in the fashion of Craig Stadler. Your downswing will be decidedly over the top of your body line, so you'll want to drop your right foot back more than the thinner-chested width player would. This is not the classic over-the-top error since it brings the club head *onto* the target line rather than *across* it. In fact, without this move, your swing would be overly in-to-out because of your closed stance and, without any club-face compensations, the ball would fly to the right of target.

TASK 4: SLOTTING THE CLUB

Your downswing starts with your left shoulder moving away from your chin as your club moves out toward the target line. Let your upper trunk rotate around your left leg while your right elbow clamps back to your side. Copy John Daly and Jack Nicklaus to learn this move. The tucking of the right elbow at the correct time is the difference between the error known as over-the-top and the resetting of the club into the slot used by the width player. The high handicapper pushes the club out toward the ball to start the down-swing and it just keeps going—the right elbow never tucks. The width player starts the club out toward the target line, and then, as soon as the weight shifts to the left hip, he tucks his elbow, keeping the club inside the target line.

Once your left hip is established as a pivot center, your width swing becomes predominantly right-sided—it provides the power by pushing the club to the ball in a shoveling action. Your body rotates around your left hip, using the same action that gave barrel-chested Babe Ruth his characteristic look when he hit his mammoth home runs.

TASK 5: THE DELIVERY ZONE

The W swing features the type of release in which your left hand turns over very little. When the over-the-top action is exaggerated, there's often evidence of a blocking motion (most noticeably a chicken-wing left arm) to keep the club on line longer and maintain both the loft and squareness of the club face.

As you deliver the club head, keep both heels close to the ground so your legs act as a platform for your upper body. To insure a correct approach path to the ball, let your right heel roll to the inside, toward your left, rather than flipping up onto the toe.

TASK 6: THE FINISH

Your finish is erect, in a straight-up position, with your shoulders level to the ground, a result of the club having traveled around and out during your downswing rather than down and under. Your head should be over your left foot with no bend in your back.

Summary of Width Swing

As a W player, you're bent from the hips at address with a spine angle that allows room for your arms to swing *over* rather then *around* the chest. During your backswing your arms swing as the left

Even though the weight shifted left long ago, the right foot is still down, a position that helps the width player turn into the ball with his upper body. When that right heel flips early, it pushes the right side around too quickly, steering the ball to the left.

hand pushes down on the butt of the club and the right hand pushes the club away from you along the toe line.

As part of your takeaway, your left shoulder moves behind the ball as the weight moves to your right hip joint. The key width move is allowing your upper spine to float slightly toward your right foot as you set the club in position.

During the downswing your spine floats back to its original position as the right side moves around and then forward toward the target as though you were throwing a ball underhanded. Your club is released to the ball with an upper-body punching action. While the L swing has the look of very passive hands through the hitting zone, and the A swing looks very handsy, the W swing looks armsy. A key width concept is that your lower body is a platform used by the upper body as it goes about its business of giving the ball a healthy whack. Since the upper body is in control, it's a swing that looks like all shoulders and arms. In its pure form the width swing is a short swing with a fast tempo.

WIDTH POWER LEAKS

The Float. As a muscular-advantage player you swing the club away in the width dimension, and because your chest is large, you must allow your head and upper spine to float with your shoulders as you turn away from the target. A significant power leak occurs when your try to keep your head from moving because it restricts your left shoulder turn, forcing you to lift the club up rather push it away. Fixing your head will also limit the extension of your hands away from your body (which you need for power), obliging you to lift the club weakly upward.

Low Hands. At the top of your backswing, you want what we call "low hands, high club head," and to do this you must have a grip where your left hand is strong and your right hand is weak.

This encourages the unique way you cock your wrists — by pushing down on the butt of the club with the heel pad of your left hand, you elevate the club head, giving it its height. Pushing away with your right hand gives your club head its width. You can't afford "high hands, high club head" because your flexibility won't allow you to reach up that high. Remember, you're strong enough to swing short—that's why we call it muscular advantage. It's your muscles that allow you the most direct power route to the ball.

Hip Switch. Starting your downswing means transferring your weight into your left hip joint. If you leave your weight in your right hip, the club gets too steep. Your lower body is a platform for your powerful upper body, but you must be in the correct axis (your left hip) to shallow out your swing arc so you don't hit the ball fat: the ultimate power leak.

Exceeding Flexibility. Because of chest size, flexibility, and arm length, you are limited in the depth or the "behind" dimension as well as the height or "up" dimension. If you try to swing club like the leverage player, your left arm runs into the chest too early. To continue the swing, you have to take club outside and lift it off the plane angle. We've already seen that when you exceed your flexibility in the height dimension, your body is forced to tilt back toward the target as the club nears the top of the swing. For your most powerful swing the club moves away from your body in the width dimension with a relatively early wrist set.

Tempo. Violation of your innate tempo can cause power leaks. To understand tempo we must first understand what a swing is. The dictionary states that a swing is an uninhibited, unrestricted backward and forward motion. So anything that either restricts or interrupts this motion will ruin the swing. In reality tempo is an even movement in both directions. Power leaks develop when you try to speed up the club head for more distance.

The problem comes from focusing on the club head instead of the source of the movement. It is the hips that must move at the same speed in both directions. It's like the skate line at the Ice Capades; the girl in the middle is the engine, she travels the same speed for every girl on the line, but as you go progressively out on the line each girl moves faster. The girl farthest from the center travels the longest dis-

Trying to swing the club high above him, this golfer has exceeded his threshold of flexibility, and it has ruined his swing, forcing him into a reverse pivot at the top of the swing. From this position impact cannot be good.

tance at the greatest speed: she is like your driver, the second farthest girl is the 3-wood, and so on until you reach the wedge, the one closest to the center girl.

Width Swing Adjustments

A thicker-chested width player such as Craig Stadler or Jim Albus will swing the club from a posture that is more bent over. The thicker the chest, the more one has to bend over to create room for arm swing. The more the player has to bend over to allow for forty-five degrees of arm swing, the more he has to close his stance to create a counterbalance and maintain equilibrium. The right elbow bend at the top of the swing is less than ninety degrees—somewhere between forty-five and seventy-five.

Because the posture is more bent over, the right leg is dropped back more for balance and turn. This means that the ball must be moved back even more to reposition it correctly. The left-hand grip is stronger to square the face from this position. The thicker the chest, the more the left arm rotates across the chest.

A thinner-chested width player like Larry Ziegler or Tom Lehman will swing the club on a flatter plane. They will have a more erect posture to prevent too much arm swing. Remember, never create a posture position that sacrifices balance. The grip will be stronger (more under the handle) for the right hand, with the stance closed only enough to create the correct amount of shoulder turn.

For those with long legs, a width swing will tend to have a little lateral motion on the downswing and will thus require offsetting measures: a more neutral grip, a wider stance, and playing the ball farther forward.

A width player with long arms will have a more erect posture and a flatter swing. The stance will be square to keep the club head from getting too deep behind him during the backswing. The erect posture produces a flatter shoulder turn, which coincides with the flatter plane.

A width player with shorter arms creates a posture that is bent over more, with more knee flex than normal. The stance will be closed more (about an inch for each inch by which the arms are shorter than average). The shorter arms will require a more upright swing. The posture will create an earlier setting of the wrist and a steeper shoulder turn, making the swing more upright.

A width player with a long trunk or short legs will require a more erect posture to maintain balance. He will require a ball position that is farther back to offset the exaggerated movement of the upper body off the ball.

Senior width players are usually former leverage or arc players who have lost flexibility. By adopting a stronger left-hand grip, moving the ball back, and dropping the right foot back, you set yourself up to regain the power and consistency you have lost.

Touring pro Larry Ziegler is a thick-chested width player with long legs.

LAWs Chart

	Leverage	Arc	Width 1	Width 2
Type	Meso	Ecto	Endo-MA	Normal-W
DD	depth	height	width	width
DPS	levers	length of arc	strength	combo
	mech. adv.	pos. adv.	mus. adv.	combo

The Setup

	Leverage	Arc	Width 1	Width 2
Left foot	slight flare	flare to square	flared	flared
Right foot	slight flare	90 degrees to line	flared	flared
Stance	square	square	closed	closed
Grip	neutral-MT	weak-ST	strong-LT	very strong-LT
	shaft–45 degrees	shaft-diagonal	shaft–90 degrees	shaft–90 degrees
Knees	over ankles in direction of toes	pinched in	matching direction of toes	matching direction of toes
Fanny	out	up	down/out	down/out
Spine tilt	normal	upright	bent over	bent over
Left arm	on top chest	on side	on top	well on top
Right arm	elbow to toe line	elbows to hips	elbow to target line	same
Aim	at target	right of target	right of target	right of target
Ball position	normal	forward	back	back

(continued)

LAWs Chart (continued)

	Leverage	Arc	The Swing Width 1	Width 2
Takeaway	sequential	one piece	one piece	sequential
Left arm crawl	triangle	triangle	left shoulder	left shoulder
Wrist cock	at hip high	later	hip high	early
Right wrist	concave	straight	straight	concave
Left wrist	straight	concave	concave	concave
BS axis	right hip/spine	top of spine	right hip	right hip
Elbow fold	backward	upward	outward	outward
Hip-top	level	right higher	level	level
Left arm-top	diagonal to right shoulder	above right shoulder	below right shoulder	above right shoulder
Right elbow-top	on plane	over plane	over plane	on plane
Right leg-top	flexed	straight	flexed	slight flex
Left knee-top	at ball	behind ball	in front of ball	behind ball
Shaft-top	on plane	above plane	above plane	above plane

(continued)

LAWs Chart (continued)

Starting Down

	Leverage	Arc	Width 1	Width 2
Left arm	drop/down	drop/behind	drop/outward	drop/outward
Right arm	straightens	stays bent	bent/tilts	bent/tilts
Left knee	moves back over left angle	moves outward	moves back over left ankle	stays put
Axis	Left hip/spine	top of spine	left hip	left hip
Knees	flexed	right knee straight	flexed	flexed
Halfway down				
shaft	on plane	on plane	on plane	on plane
Axis	Left hip/spine	TOS	left hip	left hip
Hips	opening	closed	open	open
Knees	flexed/bowed	flexed/close	flexed/chasing	flexed/chasing
Impact	all the same			
Finish	sideways C	reverse C	I position	I position

Legend:
TOS=top of spine
TA=takeaway
MT, LT, ST=medium, long, short thumb
DD=dominant dimension
DPS=dominant power source

7

Learning the LAWs

Drills, Aids, Fitness

In this chapter you'll find a series of drills that will allow you to link feel with technique. You can use these drills initially to learn your LAWs swing and then use them alone or in combination whenever your swing begins to slip a bit.

Leverage-Swing Drills and Teaching Aids

LEFT-SHOULDER/RIGHT-HIP DRILL

In a leverage golf swing, the first move is a simultaneous motion in which the right hip turns back over the right heel while the left arm swings forty-five degrees across the chest. The arm swing pulls the left shoulder down and the right shoulder up, allowing the shoulders to have the proper amount of incline as they rotate around the spine. To capture the feeling of this action, simply place your right hand on your left shoulder and pull down with a gentle tug. As you do, your left knee will rotate in toward the right heel, and your right hip will turn automatically over the right heel.

The feel of coil.

LEFT-ARM STRETCH DRILL

Without using a club, create your golf posture while kneeling on both knees. Grip an imaginary club with your left hand, and then put your right hand across your body and hook it underneath your left elbow (the palm of the right hand should be facing the target, while the back of the hand should be flexed back on itself to hook the left arm). From this position, simply pull your left arm across your chest to the top of the swing. This drill teaches two important lessons: it creates the feel of the proper sequence of upper and lower body found in the leverage golf swing, and the kneeling gives you a better feel for how the coil is developed.

SURGICAL TUBING TO DEVELOP COIL, STRETCH, AND PROPER SEQUENCE

Take six feet of $\frac{1}{4}$-inch-diameter surgical tubing (you can buy it at your local medical supply store), place one end under your left foot, and then loop the other end underneath the grip of your club so you can grip the tubing with no slack in it. From this position, simply swing the left arm across the chest, and feel the resistance provided by the tubing as the club swings the shaft to the top of the back-swing. You can swing only so far until the larger muscles of the back and shoulders take over to complete the motion to the top. Even though you don't actively turn the shoulders in a leverage swing (they are turned by the pull of the arm swing), this drill sets up the proper sequence and allows you to create the proper arm stretch and coil; it also eliminates the early turn of the shoulders, which is a great destroyer of the L swing.

CREATING THE WINDOW DRILL

Plant a shaft in the ground outside your left foot so that it runs diagonally across your left foot to the inside of your left knee. This technique will keep your left foot planted and prevent your left knee from collapsing. Then take a head cover and place it under your right armpit. Now swing your left arm across your chest, allowing the arm swing to coil your shoulders against your lower body. The head cover should drop from under the right arm during the takeaway as your right arm moves away from your right side creating the window and keeping the club on plane. You can even hit balls doing this drill.

PUMP DRILL

The pump drill develops the correct sequence in the downswing. At the top of the swing, initiate the downswing by turning your left hip back over your left heel while keeping the right hip over the right heel. At the same time bring your arms down in front of your body to a point where your club is parallel to the ground. Make sure to keep your arms in front of your body with the left arm maintaining connection with the chest as you do this. Go back to the top and pump the club gently up and down several times; on the third pump, hit the shot. You'll feel how the upper and lower body combine to bring the club head to the ball.

STAYING-BACK DRILL

During your downswing, your arms need time to drop, and this drill teaches you to coordinate your right-side rotation with your arm swing. To get the feel of this delayed right side, exaggerate the flare in your right foot to fifty degrees in order to heighten the sensation of how your knees separate during the downswing, a movement that gives the L player a bowlegged look at this point in the swing. Hit balls doing this drill. Note that while your weight shifts to your left hip to start the downswing, your right side doesn't start to rotate until the club drops down.

BUTT BOARD

This drill focuses on the use of your hips in the leverage swing. First, place a chair directly behind your rear end so that both cheeks contact the chair. Now take some gentle practice swings, keeping your right butt cheek snug against the chair. On the downswing the right cheek should stay in position until the left cheek returns to the chair. If you have trouble maintaining contact with the right side, flare your right foot more. Add the pump drill to incorporate the proper upper-body action. Hit balls doing this drill.

THE 8–9–10 DRILL

This drill teaches the proper sequencing of the backswing (first this happens, then that) so you can keep your club shaft at the correct angle to the ground as you swing. While it might seem complicated, stick with it, because it's a good one.

For this drill you'll need four golf clubs and a golf ball in your right front pocket. Lay the first club on the ground to represent the target line (an imaginary line from the ball to the target). Assume

Keep your right cheek to the chair until the club drops into position.

your address position, and place the second club on the ground, with the grip end at your left instep and the other end touching the toes of your right foot. The third golf club should be parallel to the target line, extending down your toe line to the right of your right foot. Now fix the grip end of your fourth club against your left hip and choke down on the club, with your right index finger extending down the shaft.

Swing your left arm across your chest, tracing the target line shaft with your right index finger until the club you are holding is directly over the shaft on the ground (left heel to right toes). While your arms are swinging, the right hip should turn back until the ball in your pocket is over the right heel. This is the eight o'clock position, and it

A perfect angle for the club of the leverage player.

represents the total amount of arm swing in the backswing. Next, go back to your address position, and swing your left arm across your chest, allowing the shoulders to turn until the club shaft is parallel to the ground, directly over the shaft along the toe line (the nine o'clock position). Now return to the address position, and swing your left arm across the chest until it pulls the shoulders around and causes your right arm to fold, a position in which your left arm is parallel with the ground and the grip end of the club is pointed at the target line (the ten o'clock position). Repeat in sequence until you can flow automatically through each position perfectly, one after the other. Remember, the shafts on the ground represent checkpoints during the swing motion. Each interval should be achieved through motion, not by placement.

Arc-Swing Drills and Teaching Aids

PUSH BACK DRILL

When your hands or arms open the club face excessively, you have to make a compensation during the downswing. Tee up a ball and, using a 5-iron, place a two-by-four on the target line directly behind the ball, leaving enough space for the club head. Now take your setup and push the board back by swinging your club head away from the ball. The weight of the board prevents you from unnecessarily opening the club face in the backswing. It also gives you the feeling of using the big muscles of your shoulders and chest to move the club head during your one-piece takeaway.

ONE-PIECE TAKEAWAY DRILL

This is a drill you should do daily at home. Take your normal setup, and then place the butt end of the grip against your belly button. Extend both arms, gripping down on the shaft as close to the club head as is comfortable. Now move everything by turning your chest away from the target. Once the club is over your right foot, simply fold the right arm to the top of your takeaway to complete the exercise. This gives you the feeling of the one-piece takeaway characteristic of the A swing.

DOWNSWING DRILL

To feel what it's like to bump the hips and slot the club on the downswing, do the takeaway drill, but add a head cover to the club head, and stand with your heels about four inches away from a wall. Now make the correct takeaway, and once the club is at the top, allow your hips to move laterally, which will cause your club head to slide down the wall.

SOCCER BALL DRILL

Place a volleyball or a soccer ball between your arms, and work on a one-piece takeaway. The ball between the arms will unite the

Getting the feel of the chest as the master mover.

shoulders and the arms, giving you the correct feel of the one-piece takeaway.

ARC POLE DRILL

Take three shafts and wrap them together with tape, which will create the teaching aid that we call an arc pole. Stick the pole in the ground about the length of a 5-iron away from your right foot and along the ball-of-your-foot line. This position represents where the golf club should begin to elevate in the backswing. Take the club back, using a one-piece takeaway until it is parallel to the ground and your club shaft is resting against the arc pole. From this key position the club will ride up the pole to the top of your swing. For the first few repetitions use this as a backswing drill. Once you feel comfortable with it, begin to swing the club down to the inside of the pole in slow motion. If you've never slotted the club like this before, it will feel like a big loop, but in reality the club is only moving a few inches into the depth dimension.

BUMP DRILL

Place a club on the ground stretching from your right heel to your left toe. This position represents the path that your hips travel at the

On the backswing the club slides up the outside of the pole; on the downswing it travels from the inside. It feels like a loop, but actually the hands don't loop the club; the lower-body action does it, if you're set up correctly. But the pole will introduce you to the arc players' figure eight.

start of the arc downswing, before they start to rotate. Place another shaft across the top of your thighs, anchoring it with both hands. Now turn your hips back until the right leg straightens but doesn't lock and the weight moves to the inside of the right foot. From this position you're ready to bump your hips along the line established by the shaft on the ground. Once your weight reaches the ball of the left foot, rotate your left hip behind you. This drill teaches the lower-body action of the arc player. Start out doing this drill in slow motion. As you become more proficient, do the drill at the speed you would hit the ball.

SHOULDER-TURN DRILL

Take a long arc pole and place it outside the ball, running diagonally past the left side of your neck; make sure that it's covered with a thick head cover for safety. Take a few swings in slow motion so that your shoulders turn under the pole. This drill will teach you how the shoulders should work in your arc swing.

WEIGHT-SHIFT DRILL

Place a wedge (facedown) under the outside edge of your right foot. As you shift weight to your right side during the backswing, the club insures that the weight will shift to the inside of your right foot. With your weight correctly positioned at the top of the swing, you've set the stage for your hip bump.

Width-Swing Drills

TUCK DRILL

This drill will require the assistance of a friend. With your friend's hand on your left shoulder, start down with the lower body, but don't move forward. This maneuver will increase the tuck of your right elbow and allow your club head to approach the ball from the inside of the target line.

The club head under the right foot creates a post out of the right leg for the upper body to coil around.

SET DRILL

Hold the club with your hands about three inches apart. Push down with the left hand and out with the right hand as you turn back. This will push the right shoulder back and will put you in the proper position at the top.

WIDTH DRILL WITH SURGICAL TUBING

Everything we do in the width swing is designed to develop width during the backswing. This drill keeps the arms out in front of the body. Take a six-foot length of ¹/₄-inch-diameter surgical tubing and tie it around your chest. Tie it at the front center of your chest, and then bring the remaining tubing to the grip end of the club. Loop it behind the handle from underneath. Grip the club and tubing, making sure to take all the slack out. Take your setup and then turn back, pushing the handle down and away from you. The tubing will offer resistance to the arms and keep them wide and in front of the body.

BOARD DRILL FOR TURN

If the arms don't do their job, the shoulders will tilt in an effort to elevate the club. Both the hips and the shoulder need to turn on their respective planes. This drill levels out the turn of the shoulders dur-

Using the tubing, you'll get the feeling of the hands pushing down and away from the body but directly in the center of his chest, a key width position.

ing the backswing, helps remove any tilting of the shoulders, and gives you feedback if your club head gets dangerously outside the target line on the downswing. Tee up a ball and place a board on the ground about one grip-width away from the ball, parallel to the target line. Now place the club head on top of the board. Turn your shoulder behind the ball as you swing the club back and hit the shot.

STORK DRILL

Take your setup, and then drop the right foot back far enough so that the toes of the right foot are touching the ground. From this position begin to hit shots. This drill requires that you rotate, not slide, on the left hip joint in order to keep your balance. It also teaches you how to drop the arms and slot the club as the upper body stays behind the ball at impact.

Drills help to lay down the tracks of learning, training the neural networks in the brain that dictate our behavior—we call them habits. But in addition to knowing how to learn the LAWs, you have to be physically able to learn them. So we've included a section on physical fitness to give you a bit of direction.

Physical Fitness for Golf

With the exception of Gary Player, Arnold Palmer, and a few others, golfers in the past were not looked upon as well-conditioned athletes. One famous golfer of yesteryear said that he didn't like to jog because the ice cubes kept falling out of his scotch glass. Another, when asked how he stayed in shape, bragged that he never lifted anything heavier than a petticoat.

But things have changed dramatically in recent years, and working out for golf is now fashionable. Instead of meeting at the bar or hanging around the locker room drinking, smoking, and playing cards, many of today's tour players meet in the fitness trailer, order room service, do their sit-ups, and go to bed early. And to preserve their

Gary Player was one of the first golfers to realize the value of physical fitness. And even in his sixties he's still superbly fit.

health, many don't smoke, either. With the rich purses, the longevity of earning power thanks to the Senior Tour, and the stiff competition, pro golfers know they need to hit it as long and straight as possible, and this means getting serious about their golfing physical fitness. The same applies to anyone, pro or amateur, who is using the LAWs model to build or rebuild his or her golf swing. Science has spoken loudly and clearly: to maximize your golf performance, you have to get fit and stay fit.

But let's be realistic: except for a certain few, most golfers are not going to put in a lot of gym time, even if it's good for their golf game. We've seen so many golfers with good intentions launch into a workout program designed by an expert who is used to spending eight hours a day in the gym. Unfortunately, that well-intentioned golfer lasts about three weeks and then quits and does no more exercising, figuring that if he or she can't do it right, they might as well not do it at all. Our message is that you don't have to spend grueling hours in the gym, hours you can't afford, expending energy you don't have, just to get golf strong.

We've designed a golf strengthening and flexibility program that takes about forty minutes. For the first six weeks do it three times a week, and then, if you have to, you can drop to two times a week. Please be aware that we are not advocating a minimum amount of exercise. Quite to the contrary, we are firm believers in maximum fitness—if it were realistic, we'd want you in the gym every day, working out under the supervision of a personal trainer who could specially design a golf-specific program to work every muscle and joint in your body. And we'd throw in a sports psychologist, a nutritionist, and a special club-fitting program, too. Maybe even a shaman to exorcise any golf demons that might have sneaked in during the rest periods. But since this isn't realistic for most, here's a forty-minute, blue-collar workout that will do you just fine.

There are just a few basic things to remember. You have to build speed by doing speed movements such as swinging a shaft with no head as fast as you can. You have to build strength by doing weight training. And you should take time to make an honest strength/weakness profile and then allocate your workout accordingly. Most of this is common sense—if you're very strong but inflexible, work on your flexibility. If you're as thin as a scarecrow, spend time lifting weights. If you're strong and flexible, maintain it and improve your cardiovascular fitness. If you're weak and inflexible, you need it all.

STRENGTH

Hips/Thighs (Hamstrings/Quadriceps). Your hips and thighs provide stabilization and turning speed in your golf swing. To develop them, use one of the exercises that Greg Norman swears by, called wall sits. Assume a simulated sitting position by anchoring your back against a wall so that your thighs are parallel to the floor. Hold this position for fifteen seconds. Do it at least ten times.

Rotators. Four tendons make up the rotator cuff, a part of the body that anchors four large muscles from the shoulder blade to the humerus bone in your upper arm. The rotator cuff holds the shoulder together and allows a very large range of motion, making the shoulder joint one of the most all-purpose joints in the body. Using very light weights, raise your arms straight away from your sides to a level just below your shoulders. Do two sets (three if you have time) of twelve reps.

Triceps/Biceps. The triceps extend your arms, while the biceps flex them. Together, they make up what is called an antagonistic muscle pair. Remember that muscles pull in only one direction when they contract, so there must be two groups to provide movement in both directions. To keep yourself in balance, take care always to exercise both muscles in the antagonistic pair. Your triceps help you to sling the club into the ball, while your right biceps folds the club during the backswing. For your bi/tri pair, do curls and extensions, two sets of twelve reps.

Pecs/Lats. Your pectorals and latissimus dorsi are big muscles on your chest and back that play a huge role in your golf swing. The left lat helps rotate your left arm counterclockwise, moving it down and across your chest during your downswing, while the left pec moves your left arm in the opposite direction, toward the midline of your body. Your left lat pulls the club down, while the role of the left pec in the downswing is to put the brakes on the left arm, slowing it down as it approaches the hitting area so that energy can be delivered down the shaft and into the ball.

The best way to work these big muscle groups is by using the bench press and the lat machine; you'll find directions for both in the gym. If you can't get to the gym, do pushups for your pecs. To work the lats, bend over until your body is parallel with the ground and anchor your head on a table. Use a gallon jug of water as a weight and lift it by trying to touch your shoulder blades together. Do two sets of twenty or thirty reps.

Hands/Forearms. You'll rarely see a pro golfer who doesn't have the strong forearms and hands needed to control the club without squeezing it to death. In your forty-minute workout, you can save time if you keep a soft, palm-size rubber ball near your desk, in your car, or next to your TV. Roll it through your fingers and squeeze it in your palms, making sure to change hands frequently to avoid repetitive-stress syndrome. In a couple of weeks, your grip will be viselike.

There is a lot more that you can add to your workout, but the exercises above combined with your stretching will take you about forty minutes. Below are some general things you should know about flexibility, which will help you stay matched to your LAWs swing.

FLEXIBILITY

In golf, strength without flexibility is like locking the genie in the bottle. Flexibility, for our purposes, is defined as the range of motion of any given joint. Flexible joints use less energy, are more efficient, and are injured less frequently. There is an increased supply of blood to a flexible joint, and the temperature of a healthy joint is higher than that of an unhealthy one, giving it greater elasticity. Flexibility training is also important because with it the nerve impulse necessary for muscle contraction takes less time to travel from the muscles to the brain and back again, thereby improving your coordination and reaction time.

Studies show that the age-induced decline in flexibility, about 10 percent per decade, can be slowed dramatically with a regular stretching routine.

NOTE: As with all fitness recommendations in this book, get your doctor's approval before you start.

GENERAL FLEXIBILITY STRETCH

1. Spread your legs about shoulder width, and without bouncing slowly bend downward from your hips until you can bend no more. Stay there for thirty seconds, allowing your body weight to stretch you out. Keep your knees slightly flexed, and please remember: never bounce up and down to get more stretch.

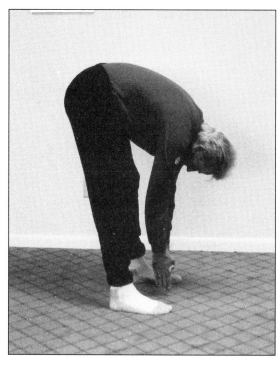

Let the weight of your upper body stretch you at the hip joints.

2. Stretch to your full height with your arms fully extended over your head and your hands together. Bend backward from the waist as far as you can, and hold for ten seconds; then straighten up, bend down, and grab your ankles. Hold for ten seconds, and then extend your hands onto the floor and form an inverted V with your body. Hold for ten seconds, and then get on all fours and stretch like a cat by pushing your fanny up, stomach down, and your head back. Now arch your back and alternate positions (fanny out/fanny in ten times). Go back into your inverted V, hold, and then hold your ankles for ten seconds; then go back up to your beginning position and hold. (Do as many as you have time for.)

THE SIXTY SECOND STRETCH: BOTH SIDES NOW

Lay a club or a broomstick across the back of your shoulders, and anchor your head against a doorjamb or the corner of a wall. Assume your golf posture, just as though you were going to hit a ball. Gradually turn away and coil, keeping your golf posture, and when you can turn no farther, hold for thirty seconds. Now reverse it and hold your impact position for thirty seconds. These two stretches work both sides of the body: your stretch at the top of the swing and your position at impact.

The key is to be in your golf posture, with your weight in the right hip for the backswing exercise and in the left for the downswing exercise.

LAWS SPECIFIC STRETCHES

Leverage/Mesomorph. As a standard mesomorph, you have moderate-to-high muscle and low-to-medium fat ratios; in other words, you're relatively high in muscle and low in fat. Your flexibility is adequate to excellent, and you tend to be on a maintenance program with two to three workouts a week. You should do some light stretching every day, including the both-sides-now LAWs staples outlined above. Do low weights with medium repetitions (ten to twelve). Since you don't need more muscle and don't want to risk injury, stay away from low reps and heavy weights. Squeeze the rubber ball mentioned in the general section, and, if you have time, do some cardiovascular work.

Arc/Ectomorph. You could use some muscle. That doesn't mean that we want you to become inflexible, but you should spend your workout time building power through a weight program designed to beef up your upper-body strength.

Muscular Advantage/Endomorph. You have strength, but flexibility is what you need. Spend most of your time doing double and triple the number of flexibility reps recommended in the general stretching program. If it says do one rep and hold for thirty seconds, do three. If you do any strength training, do very light weights and high reps.

Focus on your wrists to make them more flexible, and roll that ball around and through your fingers to make them more flexible.

8

How to Customize Your Swing

In the LAWs model, a hybrid is a sound and effective golf swing that has elements of one swing type successfully mixed with elements of another. In this chapter we'll show how hybrids develop and how to avoid becoming a "golfing Frankenstein," a mismatch of swing parts that gives you nothing but heartache. We'll outline the combinations of swing elements that just don't fit together. We'll also provide a reference section, the LAWs matching theory, to show you how certain combinations of swing elements can work together.

The golf swing is made up of many swing elements such as grip, posture, ball position, and takeaway. The question is how to put these elements together to play your best golf if your body doesn't match perfectly to the prototype. Our answer is that you begin with the LAWs and try to match your swing model perfectly, a process we call driving yourself to the perfect. Once you've adjusted to the model, then it's time to adjust the model to you by customizing your swing, using ball flight as your guide. How you shape the model to fit you depends on variations such as the conditions of play, individual differences in strength and flexibility, temperament, and a host of other natural tendencies and external influences.

As we wrote in our first book in 1996, this cross-pollination of swing elements (elements of one swing type blended with another) exists because good golf swings, in order to satisfy the laws of physics (which they all must do), evolve based on body type, personality, the demands of the environment, and often the influence of a teacher who may or may not have considered the student's physical traits.

The Continuum

A major tenet of our model is that most people are a blend of the three basic body types, with one type usually dominant. So at first glance you might think that the golfer is a mesomorph, the balanced body type of a leverage player, yet on closer inspection you find he has the long arms and the exceptional flexibility characteristic of an ectomorph arc player. Similarly, you might have a tall, thin ectomorph who uses the width swing because of uncharacteristic inflexibility or a width player who is more flexible than strong and therefore uses the leverage swing. Basically, to build a golf swing that works, you find swing elements that fit together based on what your body demands.

While all golf swings are a blend of up, down, and around, each swing type has a characteristic look because of the predominance of one dimension (height, width, or depth) in the blend. So the impression you get from the arc swing of someone like Fred Couples or Davis Love is "long and high and reaching for the sky." Overall, these swings look quite different from the rotational action of players such as David Frost, Mark O'Meara, or Chip Beck. They might be described as "around and around with a swish in the middle." And when you see Duffy Waldorf or Craig Stadler crush it, it strikes you as "short, back, and through with lots of hit." What you are seeing is the golfer's dominant dimension stealing the visual scene.

When we present the three basic swing types of the LAWs of golf to our students or fellow professionals, invariably we're asked the following question: "How do you explain the fact that many tour players have traits of two swing types mixed together?" The answer reveals the power of the model as a teaching and learning tool.

As we have said, in real life few golfers are an identical match to the pure prototypes we've depicted. Thus, the most accurate way to interpret the model is to create a triangle with one of the three pure swing types at each of its points. The points represent each prototype, the corresponding swing type, and its mechanics: the pure arc swing, the pure leverage swing, and the pure width swing. Each type manifests only the characteristics of its type, with no elements of the other types included.

To customize your swing, you should understand the concept of the continuum of traits. It might help to think of the continuum as a color scale that has nuances of color ranging from white to jet black, with many shades in between. There is then a visual continuum that becomes apparent once you are familiar with the LAWs model—in other words, simple observation can reveal many answers.

The diagram of the LAWs on paper is as follows. We envision a continuum constructed like a triangle, with the sides of the triangle connecting the prototypes. They produce an arc to width, an arc to leverage, and a leverage to width connection. As characteristics of another swing type are added or subtracted (e.g., wrist cock, takeaway, hip action), the swing type slides back and forth, either approaching or moving away from its pure prototype.

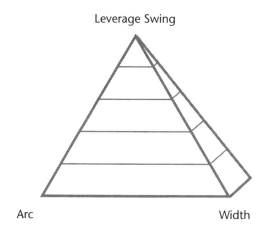

Leverage Swing

Arc   Width

The Hybrid

169

Since the LAWs model is designed to be shaped to the individual, you should further customize your swing by making modifications that fit you specifically. To do so, you'll add particulars of one swing type to yours as you migrate along the continuum toward the midpoint, the blending that we call a hybrid. The designations of the hybrid are categorized as follows:

L-A: a leverage player with some arc characteristics
L-W: a leverage player with some width characteristics
A-L: an arc player with some leverage characteristics
A-W: an arc player with some width characteristics
W-L: a width player with some leverage characteristics
W-A: a width player with some arc characteristics

The hybrid swing is composed of a dominant swing type with contributions from another swing type that fits a player's individual body type and enhances his shot-making ability. For example, an arc player who has some physical characteristics of a width player might incorporate a few swing elements of the width swing into his predominantly arc swing. They are not compensations in the negative sense in that one makes up for or corrects the other. Rather, they are synergistic enhancements, where the strength of the one is multiplied by the presence of the other.

The swings of a young Jack Nicklaus and Ian Woosnam are examples of hybrids. Nicklaus in his prime was an A-W hybrid. He—like the present-day king of the A-W hybrids, John Daly—had the thick chest of an endomorph that fit nicely with the flying right elbow, the unorthodox separation of his right arm from his side at the top of his swing. But the flying right elbow allowed Nicklaus to keep the primary characteristic of the arc swing that he had developed as a youth —height. A player must be very strong and supple to be a successful A-W hybrid.

The thick-chested Woosnam is an L-W hybrid whose leveraged rotary action ends in the classic muscular-advantage "I" finish governed by his flexibility and his swing path.

Please remember the following as you customize your swing type: hybrids are a natural result of shaping your swing type and your body type; when they match, you'll know it because it will be reflected in your ball flight. The fact that hybrids exist, however, is not a license to assemble any combination of swing elements haphazardly. In fact, this is a universal mistake that the LAWs model is designed to prevent. Some things, no matter how good they are on their own, just don't mix. Hot fudge goes very nicely with ice cream, but it's awful on rib-eye steak. So take care to move as close to the pure prototype as your body allows when you're learning your swing. Unnecessary additions to the prototypes simply clutter the landscape.

Most good players are hybrids, with very few exhibiting a pure swing type. Some examples of those who come very close to the prototypes are Payne Stewart (arc), David Frost (leverage), and Craig Stadler (width).

Even though our goal is to drive toward the perfect prototype, most people do not have all the physical characteristics to do so. A blending of two different swing types can be successful if the player's physical makeup dictates it. If you cared to, you could create a triangle for each player on the tour. Here are several to give you the flavor of the concept.

Fred Couples and Greg Norman are both blends of arc and leverage; they differ in that Norman is predominately a leverage player with arc tendencies, while Couples is an arc player with leverage tendencies. John Daly and Tom Lehman are excellent examples of a blending of arc and width characteristics; Tom Kite and Nick Price balance leverage and width to perfection.

Norman (6 feet, 180 pounds), for instance, has slightly longer arms than normal for his body. He's very flexible and extremely strong.

In his early days Norman copied Jack Nicklaus's one-piece takeaway, putting his hands in a very high position at the top of his swing. This meant that he needed to have a good deal of hip slide to delay his hips, so that his hands had time to get back in front of his body at impact. When he didn't, he would leave the ball to the right. To prevent this occasional error to the right and to improve his short iron play, Norman adopted a more rotational swing (the "modern" swing), but he kept his arc takeaway. To facilitate a rotary hip action and a more shallow approach to the ball, he lowered and deepened his hand position at the top of the swing.

The five-foot-eleven-inch, 185-pound Couples, on the other hand, is predominantly an arc player, but because of his thicker chest, he takes on some leverage characteristics to allow his body and swing to work in harmony. Couples learned to play with a very strong left-hand grip, and with the instincts of a great athlete, his entire swing developed to match it. His strong grip requires an earlier right-elbow fold to keep the face from shutting, and he plays the ball farther back in his stance than the average arc player. His larger chest requires him to bend more at address (leverage) to create room for his arms and body to work in harmony. At the top of his swing, he flies his right elbow, which also helps to open his club face. The strong grip at address now turns into an asset at impact, squaring up the open club face.

Thus, from the top down his swing is pure arc. With his hands so high, he has to shuttle his hips laterally to give his hands time to arrive at impact in sync with his body. The key is the speed with which his right elbow tucks back in front of his right hip. When Couples errs, it is often a time-IQ problem where his leverage tendencies take over and his hips get too rotational. When this happens, he's subject to bouts of hooking the ball and can also leave it to the right.

John Daly (five feet eleven inches, 210 pounds) is a prime example of a player built like a width player (thick chest, stocky build) whose long arms and flexibility allow him to be an arc player. His build requires that certain adjustments be made: because of his thick chest, his posture is more bent (width) and his stance is wider to maintain the balance he needs for his high-speed swing. Once he reaches the point where most width players complete their backswing, his long arms and incredible flexibility take over and elevate the club into the height dimension (arc). With his hands high above him, he has a long way to travel on the downswing, another arc characteristic that matches with his lateral hip motion.

Tom Lehman is built like an arc player: he is tall with long legs, but his thick chest and shorter arms encourage a hybrid W-A approach. His long legs move laterally (arc), a match with his forward ball position (arc). Lehman's takeaway is wide and compact (width), yet his downswing begins with a good deal of lateral hip motion (arc) combined with a tucking of his right elbow into his side (width). He also retains much of his right elbow bend well into the impact zone, a move that keeps the club face from shutting down.

Though Nick Price's build resembles that of a leverage player in many ways, his thick chest makes him predominantly a width player. His posture is a classic leverage configuration (bent from the hips, shaft and spine forming a ninety-degree angle), as is his stance width and foot flare. His backswing is classic width, with the early, wide setting of the club as he makes a three-quarters backswing. In the downswing Price has that bowlegged look of a leverage player combined with a width player's tuck of the right arm, which drops the club head into the depth dimension. His finish is a classic width "I" finish.

Tom Kite is a leverage player whose body has thickened, causing him to move the ball back in his stance, strengthen his grip, and shorten his backswing, all width adjustments. His swing is still rotary (leverage), but he finishes in the typical "I" position of the width player.

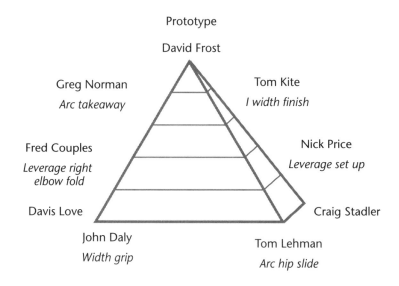

Prototype

David Frost

Greg Norman   Tom Kite
Arc takeaway   *I width finish*

Fred Couples   Nick Price
Leverage right   *Leverage set up*
elbow fold

Davis Love   Craig Stadler

John Daly   Tom Lehman
Width grip   *Arc hip slide*

As you create your own personalized triangle as part of your integration into the LAWs model, remember that the continuum of traits is not an academic concept; it is based on everyday observation. Prototypes are ideals, but hybrids are real. Prototypes are the abnormal, while hybrids are the norm. And herein lies the true value of the LAWs model: as you build your swing, you can strive for a pure prototype until you're as close as your individual body characteristics allow. Once you reach these natural limits, a hybrid results. It is only when you venture too far along the continuum, away from your basic body type, haphazardly adding parts from other swing types that don't fit, that you become a golfing Frankenstein.

Customizing Case Histories: How Hybrids Develop

By this time, you've matched the prototype. Now it's time to hit balls and monitor the ball flight to make sure that your secondary characteristics are not causing a problem. If the ball is going where you want it to, go play. If the ball is not going where you want it to, then take the second step to determine how much of a hybrid you are. Do that by going back to the LAWs identification test (LIT); look at your letters of the LAWs. You may have fourteen L's, but if the four W's you have are all in flexibility, you're an L-W hybrid who definitely needs to make some changes to the leverage model. Make them one at a time, and see how they affect your ball flight. This is how you migrate along the continuum, creating hybrid swings that match hybrid bodies. Changing your swing without the guiding hand of the model is tinkering, and this, as we have shown, produces mismatches.

CASE HISTORY 1: JOHN OF ARC

John was an aging arc player, the type we call an "Arc-iver." His LIT was almost evenly divided between A's and L's, but he had been an arc swinger for twenty-five years, and in his younger days he was as prototypical as you can get. At six feet and 165 pounds, his chest was not large, although he was strong with a lot of fast-twitch muscles fibers. He was also a very long hitter with a low handicap. His problem was that he was hitting too many shots to the right, some with a slice spin that produced the infamous right-then-more-right ball flight that no course is wide enough to hold.

When he went to his letters of the LAW, John found that his flexibility had declined to W levels so that he no longer swung the club to the high-handed arc position even though he still had the lateral hip action of the arc player. His hands had dropped but not deepened so they were getting to the ball much too soon before his hips had time to turn. This caused him to pull-hook the ball, something a good player fears above all else. To avoid the pull-hook, he began to slide so much that it moved his swing center past the ball, causing a blocking action that sent the ball to the right.

Using the LAWs model, he customized his swing as follows: he flared his back foot to give him not only lower hands but also deeper leverage hands. He moved the ball back in his stance and deflared his left foot to force his hips to turn sooner through the hitting zone. And he narrowed his stance from wide to medium to allow a more rotary swing motion. He still had his arc hip bump, but now the timing of the hip turn was matched to his hand position so that the club head arrived at impact on time. John of Arc became a hybrid by evolution, and by using the LAWs model correctly, he could adapt his swing as his body changed.

CASE HISTORY 2: ACCURATE ARTHUR

Arthur is a middle-handicap (15), middle-aged, middle-of-the-fairway golfer with a better-than-average short game who took the LIT and came up leverage. His game was driving it in the fairway, hitting it around or onto the green, and getting up and down in two. His problem was that the ball began going to the left too often, putting him in places that even his strong short game couldn't save him from.

The pull popped up unexpectedly, especially when he got tired late in the round. Arthur checked his LIT results and noticed that while his hip flexibility was leverage, the rest of his flexibility letters were W's, which meant that his upper-body flexibility no longer matched with the rest of his leverage characteristics. He could still use his hips as he needed to, but since his upper body was less flexible, with less upper-body turn, his hands couldn't get deep enough into the depth dimension. When it came time to start back to the ball, his hips worked well enough, but his hands were coming from outside his body line, and that spelled pull. He was a L-W hybrid trying to play as a pure L, and it was costing him shots.

He needed to customize his L-prototype swing by adding some width adjustments for flexibility. He had to get his hands deeper at the top of his swing without relying on his upper body turn. He made the adjustment by dropping his right foot back and flaring it. This gave him depth that did not require as much of a turn. He also moved the ball back and used the floating-coil backswing of the width swing to match his L hips and his W hands.

CASE HISTORY 3: THE IRON BRIAN

Brian is a width player, but when he swung like the prototype, he had no power, even though his letters of the LAWs were almost all W's and he was very strong. In fact, the interview revealed that he was a weight lifter whose large chest came from three-hundred-pound bench presses. Because he was into physical fitness, he knew how to lift correctly through a full range of motion, so he was not only strong but flexible, unusually so for someone with such a large upper body. When he tried to push the club back so that his hands were low and in front of him with a closed stance, as the prototype suggested, he created very little coil, and even with all his strength, the power he generated was nowhere near what he was capable of. Sensing his lack of power, he allowed his swing to become a blur of hands and arms that were moving so fast that his weight had no chance to transfer either back or through. His all-hands-and-arms swing left him stranded on legs that were like two immovable poles that impaled him in the ground.

As soon as he adjusted the model for hand position, things began to change. To create high hands, he adopted a one-piece takeaway with a very late right-arm bend. He also deflared his right foot a bit and flared his left more, moving the ball forward, and he made two very important adjustments to his stance: he squared it up and made it wider.

By making these adjustments, he gave himself the gift of time. He now had time to shift his weight, and he had a stable but dynamic platform to hit off. Now the power came from deep within him, from the big muscles of his back and thighs; instead of trying to force it, as he had done when he was mismatched, all he had to do was let the power out. Through his adjustments he had created a W-A hybrid, rare but very effective.

These are examples of how golfers can use the model to create hybrids to approach their *perfect swing*—a phrase that has a special meaning in the LAWs model.

Perfecting Your Swing: How to Use the Model to Realize Your Golfing Potential

Given the appropriate body characteristics, it would be possible to produce a pure swing type by manipulating the swing characteristics. The perfect swing is approachable if you know the model and have the matching body characteristics. Obviously, "perfect" means "perfectly suited to you"; when attained, this ideal would be a giant step in maximizing whatever talent you have for the game. So there are two very important steps that you need to take to develop your blueprint: adjusting to the model and then adjusting the model to you. This makes your swing perfect—not in an objective sense but in the only sense that really matters: perfect for you.

Adjusting the Model to Fit the Individual

In this section we offer the LAWs matching theory. At first glance, the information might seem difficult. Keep in mind, however, that this is a reference tool for making precision adjustments to your swing, to be drawn on selectively when you need it.

If this is your first experience with the LAWs model, just skim the material so that you understand the concept of matching. Later, when you've learned and implemented the fundamental swing mechanics appropriate for your body type, you can return to this chapter to further tailor your swing to your unique characteristics. This way you'll have a catalogue of specific swing adjustments, and you can refer to the section that addresses your problem.

What State Is Your Golf In?

The more you work with matching, the better you'll become at customizing and troubleshooting. If there is something wrong with the ball flight, find the mismatch and fix it. The mismatches come in many varieties: between your swing and your body type, your equipment and your strength, the target and your club face, the ball in relation to your feet, the face of the club in relation to the path or your time IQ; this last one will throw everything out of whack. If you're not hitting the ball correctly, somewhere a mismatch lurks, and the better you are at finding it, the better you'll be at golf.

We look at everything as either being mismatched, in transition, or in a state of match—that region of golf country where your best golf is played. Being in a state of mismatch is an unhealthy, troublesome, and energy-poor condition, one that can be redressed with some effort and attention.

Being in transition between mismatch and match is a chaotic, unsettling time, one of peaks and valleys in performance. The transition state is a dangerous time because you can go either way—you can sink into mismatch by tinkering, or by using the LAWs model, you can emerge into the state of match.

Our message to you is not to be put off by the chaos that surrounds the journey from mismatch to match because chaos is a sign that learning is taking place. The process of learning your golf swing (or anything else) begins when you challenge your brain by flooding it with new information: a new grip, a different aim, or a brand new start to your downswing. This informational overload creates a period of uncertainty and chaos as the perturbations of change reverberate throughout the neural pathways. At this point, to prevent itself from being overrun by the new input, the brain reorganizes itself at a higher level of complexity, one that can handle the overload.

Once the growth has occurred, the brain rewards itself by releasing pleasure molecules called endorphins—very clever of these humans to reward themselves for learning. Given our intrinsic reward system, which makes learning enjoyable, the message is clear: when you're learning the LAWs or troubleshooting your swing, the process should not approached as hard work. Golf is a game that is best learned and best played when you treat it as fun. Enjoying the game is your passport to the state of match.

The state of match is where you move your body and club through the four dimensions in perfect concert with the laws of physics. In this state energy flows from the coiling of the big muscles of the body and is then transmitted through the arms and hands, down the shaft, and emptied into the ball—and the ball, excited by this new infusion, flies to target. In the state of match, your golf swing is on automatic and can be repeated with such regularity that we say, even in the face of some bad shots, "There is a player who can golf the ball."

To be able to "golf *your* ball," you must know how to adapt your game to your body, and there are some general adjustment guidelines that will help you to accomplish this. We've laid out some matching pairs for you. When these matches are mixed with other matches, the quality of the match can, in some combinations, be problematic. Still, it is good to know them and to build and troubleshoot your blueprint with them in mind.

The LAWs Matching Theory

DIMENSIONS HAVE TIME

Before we present the matches, there is a concept you should be familiar with. It has to do with the synchronization of your swing, one of the most important elements of which is timing. To build a sound, repeatable swing, you must be aware that it is not only *what* you do but *when* you do it that's important. It's easy to confuse the two, and it can ruin your swing when you do.

Here's one way to look at it: in your golf swing, dimensions have time. The ball doesn't move away from your hands—your hands move away from the ball, and the farther away they get, the longer it takes them to get back, and that takes time. You buy a round-trip ticket with each swing, and the journey back is usually a more perilous one.

The higher your hands swing in the height dimension, the more time it takes them to get back to the ball. And the farther, or more around you, that your hands swing in the depth dimension, the more time it takes them to come back around to the ball. It's also the same with the width dimension—it also has a time factor. The shortest time between two points is also the shortest distance. Thus hands that are positioned high and away behind you are the slowest hands—in our space travel analogy, they are coming back to earth from planet Ramdon, seven galaxies away. John Daly is the prime example of a Ramdonite, with Phil Mickelson a distant second; they and others with high, deep hands must employ some major-league waiting strategies to slow their hips. This is why we say that if you have a long swing, it had better be a slow swing, because your body has to wait for your hands. It's the waiting part that makes a long swing smooth and yet so powerful.

Conversely, if you have a short swing, it will look fast if it has any substance to it at all. This is because your hips speed up by rotating sooner during the downswing, and the short distance your hands travel makes them look like lightning uncorked. Nick Price and Lanny Watkins have short swings, and it's the not-waiting part that makes them so explosive.

NOTE: Please be aware that throughout this section we'll use the word *hand* for convenience to represent the club, arms, and hands package. This may not be perfect, but it will do to explain what follows.

HIPS/HANDS PACKAGE

We often see golfers whose hand position at the top of the swing doesn't match their hip action. This may be a new concept for you, so here's one way to look at it: your hands and thus the club head

These hands have a long way to go, so the hips move laterally to "wait" for them.

must get back in front of your body in time for impact. From the top of your swing, it's a race to impact between your hands and your hips. Keep in mind that although your hands have a long way to go from the top of your swing, your hips are much closer to the finish line (your hands travel about eighteen times farther then your hips). This means you have to coordinate your hips/hands package in order for your club head to arrive at the ball when it should, full of energy and looking down the target line.

Unless otherwise noted, the words *slow* and *fast* are used here in terms of distance traveled to their appointed positions at impact. Hips that move laterally before they rotate are, in effect, slow because there is a delay before they turn—a time window that gives the hands a chance to catch up. And because they have taken the long route, it takes the hips longer to get to impact, so we call them slow. Fast hips rotate early in the downswing with only a touch of lateral movement before they turn; and because they arrive at their appointed impact position sooner, with minimal wait or delay, we call them fast.

THE STAGGERED START

You can see a good illustration of the relationship of distance and time in the staggered-start race. The runner on the outside of the curve is in the slow lane—he has to run farther, so they start him closer to the finish line. The runner on the inside is in the fast lane—his is the most direct route to the finish line. So to even it out, they start him farther from the finish line. If the runners are perfectly staggered and they all run at the same speed, they'll finish in a tie. And if your hands and hips are correctly staggered (positioned) and your timing is good, your race to the ball will end in a powerful, perfectly synchronized tie called impact.

This is an important concept that will help you to put the governor on the hit instinct—that disruptive, usually mistimed urge to pour on the power. The most powerful impact occurs not by conscious manipulation but by synchronizing your hips/hands package so that the "energy dump" from the golfer, through the shaft and into the ball, occurs on time.

The hands, then, can be thought of as being fast or slow depending on how far they travel to impact (what lane they're in). Hands that travel a long route come from positions high above and deep behind you, and they take more time to reach impact than hands that take a shorter route (fast hands) from a lower position—one where the hands are kept in the middle of the chest.

THE WAIT

Now if your hands are in a position at the top of your swing where they must travel a long distance to impact (slow-lane hands), you want your hips to have some wait in them so your hands can catch up; you want slow-lane hips, too, so that they have a long distance to go before they turn. It's just the opposite for hips that turn soon, with minimal lateral movement. If a player has no wait in his hips, his hands must be positioned on a short route to the ball; otherwise his hands will have too far to go and too little time to get there. Hips with no wait don't match with slow hands.

In light of the foregoing, you can see that slow hips and fast hands are mismatched unless you like to pull the ball way to the left. The fast hips/slow hands duo isn't any better, because your club head will be late for impact, causing the ball to go right of the target. To swing your best, you should coordinate your hands and hips so they match —slow with slow, fast with fast. There are several ways to do this.

TRICKY BUSINESS

You can focus on the hips and simply delay them or have them turn earlier to match your hand positioning. This can be done, but its difficult to get it just right because to the brain hip speed is not directly connected to club-head speed—there are too many intermediaries such as the shoulders, arms, hands, and club. That's why many golfers try to make the club go faster by lunging at the ball with their body; they simply don't know how to use their hips for power. Unfortunately, not many people can figure out how fast to turn their hips or how hip speed translates into club-head speed. So while it can be done, consciously fooling with your hip speed is a tricky business.

Another way is to focus on your hand speed. Since the club is locked to you by your hands/handle connection, your sense of feel is much more intense in your hands so you could try to speed them up or slow them down. But while this is better than tampering with your hip turn, it's not the best way to coordinate your hips/hands package because it involves a conscious adjustment, something you should avoid whenever possible.

The best way to match your hands and hips is to make setup adjustments—such as ball position and foot flare—that do it automatically for you. This way, you don't have to think about swing mechanics while you swing.

How can you tell if your hips/hands package is out of sync? Evaluate the ball flight. The ball doesn't care about the individual partners in the hip/hands package; all it cares about is impact: is the club face there on time, with the correct angle of attack and center struck, dumping energy into the ball from a club face that's looking at the target? So if the ball flies consistently to the left and nothing else is wrong, the hips — no matter how fast they look — are, in effect, too slow. Nick Price appears to have very fast hips, but most days they're not too fast because he slows them, not by consciously cutting back on their actual speed, but by sitting down to the ball just as he starts his downswing. This adjustment strategy delays his hip rotation and effectively slows his hips so his hands have time to get back in front of his body at impact. It is this move that creates the mid-downswing, bowlegged look made famous by Sam Snead.

HAND POSITIONS

Because distance is time, we can rate the hand positions at the top of the swing as follows.

Hand Position 1. The slowest hand position is the arc position, in which the hands are high over the player and there's a long club-head arc. This comes in part from the angle of the left arm, which in the prototype is above the angle of the shoulders at the top of the swing.

Hand Position 2. The next slowest hand position is the leverage position, in which the hands are lower but farther behind the body line.

Hand Position 3. The fastest hand speed is that of the width player, whose hands are low and extended away from him, in line with the middle of the chest.

Summary. High hands are slow hands—they take the longest route to reach impact, and they should be matched with late-turning hips. Low hands are fast hands, and they match with early turning hips.

You can recalibrate your hips/hands package by changing the position of your hands at the top of the swing. The slowest hands are the highest (TOP LEFT), the next slowest are the leverage hands (TOP RIGHT), and the fastest are the lowest hands, the width hands (BOTTOM).

General Adjustments for Customizing Your Swing

The single most important physical attribute for golf is flexibility—having it is no assurance that you will be a good golfer, but not having it severely limits your options. A highly flexible person can use any of the three swing types, assuming the other body characteristics match the model. Thus there are flexible arc players, flexible leverage players, and even flexible width players. But as soon as you lose your flexibility, your options are narrowed substantially. The reason for this can be seen when we look at how the dimension of time and your flexibility are related.

READER'S NOTE: There is some repetition in the following sections. We have separated certain matching pairs for study and many of their effects are the same.

MATCHING FLEXIBILITY AND TIME

Flexibility allows your hands to make a long journey, while lack of flexibility limits them to a short one. It is in this sense that time is tied to flexibility, and it's the reason why flexibility was weighted so heavily in the tests in chapter 3—time is a dimension, and in this sense flexibility is time.

Highly flexible players can swing their hands far away from their body. In the downswing, though, they sometimes have trouble delaying their hip rotation long enough for the club to get back in front of them at impact. Arc players, for example, can be victims of their own flexibility because they have difficulty coordinating their hip/hand speed. Keeping their timing at a high level requires a lot of practice, which is why we refer to the arc swing as high-maintenance.

MATCHING STANCE WIDTH AND HIP ACTION

With a wide stance, the tendency is for more lateral hip motion and later rotation of the hips. When the stance is narrow, the hips rotate sooner.

This is one of the most fundamental matchup pairs, and it can lead to very quick, seemingly miraculous cures when administered at the right time. Let's say you have matched the model in all respects, and the ball is still going to the right. You're a A-L player with decent but not great flexibility. Your stance is on the wide side, and you have a lot of lateral hip movement toward the target before your hips turn, just as the prototype dictates. But since you're not a pure arc player, the variable here is the stance width. If you narrow your stance, it will allow your hips to rotate sooner, and this will square the club up at impact. This is exactly how you should use your LAWs model: first you match the model, then you observe the ball flight. If there's a problem, you go to this reference chapter and find the matchup that will correct the ball flight. Once you institute that match, the ball flight will confirm that you have chosen the correct matchup.

MATCHING GRIP AND HIP SPEED

Squaring the club face at impact requires early turning hips that match with a strong left-hand grip. Early hip rotation in the absence of a strengthened grip results in an open club face. Hips that move more laterally before they turn match a weaker left-hand grip and more aggressive hand action to square the club face.

MATCHING HIP TURN AND DISTANCE TRAVELED

The more your hips turn both back and through, the longer their journey. One way to match your hand position with a big hip turn is to swing your hands farther above and/or behind you. Another way is to leave your hands alone and adjust your address position to restrict your turn by using less foot flare. Just the reverse is true for too little hip turn in relation to your hand position.

MATCHING BALL POSITION AND HIPS

You can learn a lot about the theory of matching from understanding the influence that ball position has on your hips/hands package. By changing the position of the ball in your stance, you are, in effect, moving the finish line (the ball) in the race to suit your purpose. So if your hips are early rotators, you can move the ball back in your stance so that your hands arrive at the ball sooner. To synchronize a swing with a late hip turn, move the ball forward to delay impact long enough for the hands to get there.

MATCHING FOOT FLARE AND RELEASE

To change the timing of your release, adjust the flare of your feet. Turning your left foot out delays the straightening of the left leg and the formation of the left wall that triggers the release. Deflaring your left foot results in a quicker release.

MATCHING STANCE WIDTH AND HIP SPEED

For hips that turn too early, widen the stance so that the rotation of the hips is delayed by adding lateral hip motion. A narrow stance encourages earlier hip rotation and less lateral motion, so the hips arrive at their impact position sooner, without much wait. This is what makes them fast in the LAWs model.

MATCHING PLANE AND BODY LENGTH

One thing that determines the height of the backswing is the length of the right forearm (elbow to thumb compared to elbow to shoulder). The longer this element is, the higher the hands are at the top of the swing. To match the high hands, the hips should move laterally before they turn. This slide-then-turn move gives the hands time to get back in front of the body. The shorter this element is, the lower the hands, and the matchup is with hips that turn sooner.

MATCHING LEG LENGTH AND ALIGNMENT

If one leg is longer than the other, one hip is higher than the other. Since it is vital that you begin your golf swing from a position of balance, you'll need to level your hips at address no matter what swing type you are. If your right leg is longer than your left, you need to close your stance until your hips are level and then match the model, using this as your starting position. If your left leg is longer, open your stance until your hips are level.

Satisfying Your Collision Requirements

A vital role of the setup is to arrange a collision between the club head and the ball. There are certain ratios that satisfy the collision requirements (CR's). This means that there are certain ratios of shoulder to hip turn, to hand distance, and to the total distance your club head travels that, when satisfied, bring the club head to the ball on time and with power.

To keep your swing in sync, you must cover distances and ratios so that all the elements are coordinated in time and space. When something in your swing changes and disrupts your ratios, your swing is no longer calibrated correctly. For example, if you tilt instead of turn your shoulders, your shoulders can't travel their allotted distance, or, if your hips slide too much, they can't get to their impact position on time — in both cases the ratios are broken, and your swing is out of sync. The result is that the collision doesn't occur when it should, and you're mismatched.

Now, you don't have to think about all this while you're swinging. This is where the LAWs is especially powerful because it shows you how to operate successfully in the four dimensions based on individual characteristics such as strength and flexibility. The point is that when you match up correctly, your CR's are satisfied automatically.

MATCHING SWING LENGTH AND BODY SPEED

Long swings rely on the length and height of the arc to build power gradually, like a 747 taxiing down the runway on takeoff. If a swing is too long, the club can't get back to impact in time, and the ball goes to the right. A lot of players come over the top when their swing gets too long — like the kid who takes a shortcut by hopping backyard fences so he won't be late for dinner, they "jump the fence" to get to the ball on time.

For power, short swings are explosive. Much like a drag race, they reach high speeds very quickly. If they get too fast, however, they actually lose power; if they're too slow, they don't generate enough power. The perfect combination is right in between.

MATCHING SWING LENGTH AND HIP MOTION

When the hands are high above you, they are slow hands that don't arrive at impact on time unless you delay your hips by moving them laterally. A long swing, in which the hands are high, doesn't match with early hip rotation during the downswing. This error, with no compensation, would send the ball to the right of the target. Hands that travel a short distance don't match with lateral hips; in this mismatch the ball goes left.

When they are late for impact, many golfers "jump the fence" to save time by shoving the club head out toward the target line. Notice how steep the shaft is: the club face will probably be open at impact.

MATCHING CLUB FACE AND HIP TURN

The more the hips move laterally before they turn (we call this hip motion slide/turn), the more time the club face has to close before it arrives at impact. Said another way, lateral hips give an open club face the time it needs to square up to the target at impact. When the club face is shut at the top of the swing (the face points to the sky), you can prevent overclosing of the club face by matching up early turning hips with very little lateral motion (rotary hips). For an already shut face, the less time it has to close, the better.

MATCHING GRIP AND RELEASE

A weak grip usually results in open club face at impact, and absent any adjustments during the downswing, the ball will slice. The open club face is due to the way the hands are placed on the club, a placement that discourages the squaring up of the club face through impact. A weak grip, therefore, requires a more hands-oriented, active release to square up the face. Conversely, a strong grip encourages toe-over-heel rotation, allowing more of a body-oriented release in which the hands are quiet. It appears to the eye that the hands are quiet even though they are actually working very well with the body to release the club face to the ball. If the grip is very strong, the release is held off by keeping the right arm bent longer, delaying the rotation of the club face. Unless there are compensations, if your grip is too weak, you'll slice the ball: if it's too strong, you'll hook the ball. The matchup is weak grip/hand release, strong grip/body release.

Two Rights Make a Wrong

When your club face comes away from the ball at the start of your swing, it's in the process of opening (pointing to the right of target). This is because your body is rotating and your right elbow is bent. Now, if you don't spin the shaft as you turn, the club face will stay square to whatever path or arc the club is moving on. In other words, your club face will be open to the target but square to its path. When you spin the shaft during the takeaway, however, you get two opens: not only is your club face pointing to the right of the target (as it should), but it's also pointing to the right of the path that it's swinging on — a mistake that can cause a mismatch. In this case, two rights make a wrong.

MATCHING GRIP AND BALL POSITION

As we have said, weak grips and forward ball positions go together —when the club face is open at the top due to the weak grip, the ball is positioned farther forward in the stance to give the club face time to close. With a weak left-hand grip and the ball back too far, the shot will fly straight right and then slice. For a strong left-hand grip the ball position is back of the standard for each swing model, a position that gives the face less time to close.

A forward ball position doesn't fit with a strong left-hand grip because the ball is on the inward part of the swing arc, and the club face is shut by the time it gets to the ball. When this error occurs, the ball flies left and then hooks farther left.

Strong Right Hand. When the right hand is in a strong position, there's usually an early wrist set with a more rotational, low-handed swing. If the right-hand grip is too strong, the club can be pulled inside the body line during the takeaway, which results in pulls and pull hooks. While it depends on the type of left-hand grip you use, in general the ball is played back in the stance with a strong right-hand grip.

Weak Right Hand. A weak right-hand position promotes a later wrist set. When it's used as part of a one-piece takeaway, it causes a more upright, high-handed swing because the back of the right hand stays looking at the sky longer during the backswing. The weaker the right hand, the more the ball should be positioned forward in the stance.

ELBOW BEND/CLUB-FACE POSITION

Both the timing and the amount of the release of the bend in the right elbow is related to the club-face position at the top of the swing. In general, players with a shut club-face at the top of the swing keep the right elbow bent longer than do open-faced players. Open-faced players straighten the right elbow more through impact. Players who draw the ball release the right elbow bend earlier, while players who fade the ball hold the bend longer.

MATCHING POSTURE AND SWING PLANE

The more you bend from your hip joints, the greater your spine angle and the more upright your swing will be with more shoulder angle. The more erect your posture, the more it matches a rounded swing with a flatter shoulder turn.

MATCHING FOOT FLARE AND RELEASE

The more flare in the left foot, the later the release; the less the left foot is turned out, the earlier the release.

Foot flare is one of the most important matches in the LAWs model because it deals directly with impact. The release of the angles of power are completed as soon as the left side wall is set up. If done correctly, the release is passive because leverage is released as a result of running into the wall. The release is passive in the sense that you don't "do" one — you "have" one. Imagine a horse and rider approaching a six-foot wall at full gallop; suddenly the horse stops, but the rider continues over the wall. In our analogy the horse is the arms/hands unit, the wall is the left leg, and the rider is the club head. If the wall is farther down the trail, the collision occurs later; if it is farther up the trail, the collision occurs sooner. But in order for the release to be correct, it must be triggered by the left wall. If the wall is poorly formed, the release will be weak and mistimed.

Right-Foot Flare. The flare of the right foot affects the shape of your swing. The more the right foot flares, the more rounded the swing; the less flare, the more upright the swing.

MATCHING THICK CHEST AND POSTURE

A broad, thick chest requires a posture with more spine tilt. If a player with these characteristics is matched correctly, he'll have more bend from the hips and less knee flex than usual. The correct posture allows the club to be pushed away from the chest while the hands remain in the center of the chest.

Hitting across a firm left leg releases the club to the ball. Because you don't make it happen, you let it happen; we call it a passive release.

MATCHING THIN CHEST AND POSTURE

A player with a thin chest requires a more erect spine (less hip bend) with a bit more knee flex. The club is swung more around on a flatter plane angle. This seems to contradict the match for the arc player, but remember that the priority is always to arrange yourself at address so you have forty-five degrees of arm swing. By keeping the right elbow straight during the one-piece takeaway with the back of the right hand to the sky, the arc player neutralizes the tendency to swing on a flatter plane that would normally be present due to the upright posture. Thus the club swings on an upright angle, a better match overall for the arc player despite the upright spine at address.

MATCHING SHAFT LENGTH AND SHOULDER TILT

The longer your club, the higher the percentage of weight on your right side at address; therefore, your right shoulder is correspondingly lower than your left. Conversely, the shorter the club, the more the weight moves to the left (since you don't need as big a weight transfer for the shorter clubs) and the more level the shoulders become. With the mid-irons and a fifty-fifty distribution, the right shoulder is a tad below the left; at sixty-forty, your right shoulder is below the left by the same amount that your right hand is below your left on the grip; and with the short irons at forty-sixty, your shoulders are level. Mismatching occurs when you use the same shoulder position at address for your driver as your wedge or vice versa.

MATCHING SHOULDERS AND DISTANCE FROM THE BALL

Posture at address with the shoulder blades almost touching makes the arms effectively shorter, and you must move closer to the ball than the model dictates. If your shoulders are more rounded at address, for whatever reason, your arms are effectively longer, and you'll stand farther from the ball.

MATCHING GRIP SIZE AND POSITION IN THE HAND

Thin grips place the club more in the fingers of the hand, encouraging a handsy-looking swing, whereas thick grips are held more in the palms, producing a quiet looking, more body-orientated swing.

MATCHING ALIGNMENT AND BALL POSITION

Changing the way your feet are arranged at address affects the ball position. When you open your stance by dropping your left foot back from the toe line, the ball is farther back in your stance in relation to your body; when you close your stance (right foot back from the line), the ball is farther forward. Thus, anytime you adjust your body alignment, take care to reposition the ball: for an open stance reposition the ball forward; for a closed stance, move it back.

MATCHING GRIP PRESSURE AND WRIST COCK

When you have a short, fast swing it best matches up with firm grip pressure. When the swing is long and smooth, it goes with light grip pressure. When your swing gets too fast, lighten your grip pressure. When you're not getting back to the ball on time because your swing is too long, firm up your grip pressure.

MATCHING AMOUNT OF WRIST COCK AND HIP ROTATION

More than ninety degrees of wrist cock at the top of the swing matches with a late hip rotation. When there is less than a ninety-degree set, the hip rotation is early.

MATCHING TEMPO AND PERSONALITY

Tempo and personality must match. A hyper individual who eats, drinks, walks, and talks quickly matches a short, quick swing. A laid-back person who walks, talks, and eats slowly matches a long, smooth swing.

Using Ball Flight to Adjust the Model to You

In another section we cautioned you not to let the ball be your master while you were matching yourself to the model, but since you are now presumably approaching perfection (matching your swing prototype in every regard) and you've adjusted your model for any secondary characteristics that make you a hybrid, now the ball flight becomes your teacher: first on the practice tee, as you adjust the model to yourself, and then on the golf course, the supreme test for the quality of your matchups.

As you hit balls, look for an overall pattern. As that pattern emerges, it will lead you to the final stage of customizing your swing. To do this, you combine your knowledge of matching per the above and your ability to read your ball flight.

What follows are the basics of ball flight that are general enough to be helpful. Remember that knowing the basics of ball flight gives you only a starting point from which you can deduce the cause-and-effect relationships that characterize your LAWs golf swing.

Rule of thumb: you should hit at least sixty balls for two consecutive days to identify a pattern. Note also that what follows assumes that your aim and alignment are correct.

BALL FLIGHT AND YOUR SWING

The traditional ball flight laws have been taught for years, and they can give you some valuable feedback about what is going on at impact. It is commonly believed that path is related to the direction the ball starts in and that the club-face position at impact determines the curve of the ball, but we believe that the club face has a much greater influence on overall ball flight (perhaps as great as four to one) since it affects both curve and direction. Even though much more testing needs to be done, the flight of the ball is most helpful as a general diagnostic tool since it requires no special equipment and is a part of every shot except the whiff.

BALL FLIGHT MATCHES

Curve on the ball is sidespin that occurs when the club face looks in one direction while the path looks in another. A square club face looks in the same direction as the path on which it's moving.

WHERE TO TAP

You'll find your mismatch faster by isolating one matchup pair—let's say the ball position/club face pair—and testing it; if it's not the problem, go on to the next one until you find the match you need as reflected in the ball flight. This is a far cry from tinkering, where you have no idea what you're doing. The story is told about the customer who demands that the plumber explain his $900 bill for the three minutes it took him to fix the problem: "That's ten dollars for the hammer and eight hundred ninety dollars for knowing where to tap." The better you know the LAWs theory of matching, and the more experience you have with customizing, the more you'll know where to tap.

WHAT CAUSES WHAT

Obviously we can't discuss every cause and cure—that would be a book in itself—but here are a few examples to get you started on troubleshooting.

Ball Flight: Straight Push

The ball is pushed straight to the right of target, with no curve.

INFERENCE

The path is moving in to out in relation to the target line at impact, and the club face is square to path.

WHERE TO BEGIN

While there are many reasons why the ball goes to the right, we have chosen an example that deals with an adjustment of your hips/hands package.

When your hips rotate too early during the downswing, your right elbow doesn't have the time to get in front of your right hip, and your club is blocked from getting into the correct downswing slot. You've got a path problem because your hips turn early, making your hands late. The first adjustment is to make your hips turn later —in effect, delaying impact. This will give the club head the time it needs to get out from behind you and onto the target line. Experiment with flaring both feet. If that's not effective, work on the other partner in the hips/hands package—your hands. Since they bring the club head to the ball too late, lower your hands at the top of your swing by closing your stance and using a stronger grip. Also move the ball back so your hands can get there sooner, counteracting your early hip rotation. As soon as the ball flight is fixed, make a note of the changes and add them to your swing blueprint.

Ball Flight: Push Hook

The ball starts to the right and then curves right to the left.

INFERENCE

Your ball is going to the right and then hooking, showing that you've two problems: the face is closed to the path, and the path is to the right of target. Here is a recommendation: fix the path first because many times when you fix the path, the face will fix itself after a few swings. In any case, get the ball starting at the target even if it's hooking to the left.

WHERE TO BEGIN

Fix the path as above, and then focus on the club face. The closed-face problem could have several causes. The left wall could be established too soon because the left foot isn't flared enough. Or the club face might be shut on top (look to see if it is, using video or a friend) because of too strong a grip. Approach these one at a time, and when you find the problem, go back to the model and adjust it.

Ball Flight: Push Slice

Your ball starts to the right of the target and then curves left to right.

Because the hips have already turned, the club face is late and looking to the right of target at impact. Fast hips and slow hands don't match.

INFERENCE

The path of your club is inside to out, and the club face is open to the path.

WHERE TO BEGIN

Fix the path as above, and then focus on the matchups that affect release. Look to see if your club face is open at the top of your swing. An open face matches up with decreased left-foot flare. Also check your grip; if it's too weak, strengthen your left hand a bit. You could also be fanning the club face open. If it's none of these, once the path is fixed, move the ball forward to give the club face more time to close. And lighten your grip pressure a bit to make sure you are letting your forearms rotate as they should.

Ball Flight: Straight

Your ball goes straight to the target with correct distance and trajectory.

INFERENCE

You have satisfied your collision requirements. Remember what you did, and do it every time. Ask your golf professional to film you while you're playing well, and then keep the blueprint handy when your swing starts to go south.

Ball Flight: Hook

The ball starts at the target, but just before it gets there, it curves away to the left.

INFERENCE

Your path is good, but your club face is looking to the left of the path at impact (shut).

WHERE TO BEGIN

Check the same things you did for the shut face above.

Ball Flight: Slice

Your ball starts at the target but curves away to the right.

INFERENCE

Once again your path is good, but your club face is looking to the right.

WHERE TO BEGIN

You need to test out the same adjustments as above for the fade.

Ball Flight: Pull

The ball flies directly left of target with no curve.

INFERENCE

The face of your club is square to your club path, but the path points to the left of target.

In the leverage, arc, and width swings (except for the very large-chested MA1), the club head comes at the ball from inside as it starts down; then it goes along the body line about pocket high until it moves onto the target line a split second just before impact. As we outlined in chapter 6, the MA1 reroutes the club head a little differently because of his large chest; in his case the club head comes over the body line to start the downswing but onto the target line just before impact.

WHERE TO BEGIN

There are many causes of an out-to-in path, but a bad path most often comes from a problem with your hips/hands package. In this case start with your hips, because the odds are they are not operating correctly. Since the ball is going to the left, your hips have turned too late. This most often comes from a failure to keep the right side rotating through the shot. When you stop or slow your hips too much, your upper body turns back to the ball on its own, and the club is forced on to an out-to-in approach path where the hands get to the ball too early.

There are several adjustments you can try for this problem. The first makes your hips rotate more and earlier so that the club head can come directly onto the target line. Decrease the flare in your left foot, and move the ball back one ball width to make impact sooner. If that doesn't work, put the things you changed back in place, and, just as with the straight push to the right above, work on the other partner in the hips/hands package—your hands.

For the pull shot, the club head gets to the ball too early, so you raise your hands and position them a bit deeper at the top of the swing by using more of a one-piece takeaway with a weaker right-hand grip. This, in effect, makes them slower. The next adjustment is to deflare your right foot—that is, make it more perpendicular to the target line. This helps to drive your hands higher and makes them travel farther, giving your hips more time to turn.

Ball Flight: Pull Hook

The ball starts to the left of the target and then curves more to the left.

Slow hips and fast hands don't match. A club head that gets on an outside-to-in path looks left of target at impact.

INFERENCE

The club face is looking to the left of the path in a closed position.

WHERE TO BEGIN

Fix the path first as above, and fix the face as in the hook above.

Ball Flight: Pull Slice

The ball starts to the left of target and curves to the right.

INFERENCE

The face is open to the path.

WHERE TO BEGIN

Fix both the path and the face, using the same logic as outlined in the slice above.

Ball Flight

You're not getting solid hits and you've used impact tape or chalk to show that your contact is off-center.

WHERE TO BEGIN

Check your left arm connection to your chest to determine if you're fanning (rolling) your left arm. This type of fan disrupts your swing, causing off-center contact that saps power. Next make sure your spine angle matches the model at address and that you're maintaining it while you swing. Please remember that your arms do the up and down while your body does the around, and when the body gets into the business of the up and down, it makes the club effectively longer, leading you to hit the ball fat; when you raise up, the club length is effectively shorter, so you'll hit thin. If you're straightening your spine through impact, you'll hit the ball on the toe; if you're pitching forward at contact, you'll catch it on the heel.

Go back to the model and rematch yourself, using your prototype swing model.

Ball Flight

You're not hitting the ball as far as normal.

INFERENCE

Assuming solid contact is made, your club-head speed has decreased because you are either not producing enough coil or you have some energy leaks in your golf swing.

WHERE TO BEGIN

Check out the power leaks outlined in the previous chapters.

Magic vs. Tragic

You've customized your swing so that your swing blueprint fits you like the proverbial glass slipper. Now we'll alert you to some potholes along the road to your own personal swing system. They are divided into magic vs. tragic, mismatches that could be ruinous no matter what swing type you use.

UNDERSTANDING WHAT ERROR IS

The goal of this section is to clarify the most important LAWs concept: that while the same swing element (such as grip or posture) can be *magic* for one body type, it can also be *tragic* for another body type. Should your right leg stay fully flexed at the top of the swing? Should you use a strong grip? Is a one-piece takeaway correct? Is setting the wrists early a sound theory? The LAWs model answer is, "It depends." On what? On your body type.

As we have written elsewhere, it's fashionable to use the phrase "compensating errors" to describe any deviation from so-called perfection. The phrase is usually spoken in the sad tone reserved for someone who has a debilitating disease: "Poor thing, he has compensating errors." What would you give for the compensating error in Lee Trevino's loop, Jack Nicklaus's flying right elbow, or Paul Azinger's superstrong grip? "The odds are that if you put a bag over his head so no one would recognize him and had him hit into a net so they couldn't see the ball flight, most would change Lee Trevino's looping, push-fade swing, thereby prolonging his early career as a bag room attendant at Horizon Golf Club in El Paso, Texas."

The problem is the company the word "compensating" is keeping when it hangs around with the word "error." It makes you think that all compensations are errors, but that is hardly the case. If John Daly and Fred Couples didn't fly the right elbow, their strong left-hand grips would seriously encourage a change of profession, because the club face would be very closed at the top of their swings, leading to wild hooking.

205

So beware of someone telling you, "Your stance is too closed," or "Your ball is too far forward." You may be a width player for whom a square stance is tragic; perhaps you're an arc player whose forward ball position is magic. Please remember that they are advising you based on scrolls of received truth that lead from the belief that two plus two is always four (they're right) to the conviction that there is only one way to make a golf swing (they're wrong). Our model shows you that in many cases there is no objective answer that fits all because try as some might, the certitude of mathematics is not available to us—it depends on your individual characteristics. This concept of relative right and wrong, though sour for some, should be nectar to you because it gives you a way to sort out the many pieces of advice that float your way. One wag has described life this way: the air is filled with plums and turds whizzing past us, and our goal is to dodge the turds and catch the plums. Advice about your golf swing comes whizzing at you all the time, and we think that the LAWs model, if used correctly, will help you bag your limit of plums. Here we see the value of a gatekeeper.

The presence of a gatekeeper, like a trusted teacher or a powerful swing model to which you are doggedly committed, protects your golf game from just plain bad advice as well as from good advice that doesn't apply to you. Absence of such a prophylactic has destroyed some fine players, turning many a prince into a frog.

PRINCES INTO FROGS

Once such prince was a very successful tour player who turned into a frog when he went to an instructor who inserted a leverage-style takeaway into his arc-style swing, creating a deadly mismatch. The player retained his arc lower-body move, but since his new takeaway put him in a leverage position at the top of his swing, his club came back to the ball on an incorrect path. Despite his immense talent, in a few short months he slid from one of the best players in the world to missing every cut. After much self-doubt he went back to his old swing, thereby ridding himself of his mismatch; he immediately became a contender again.

In his quest to get better, a player dubbed the "next Nicklaus" got worse instead. He was a highly successful width player who sought out the advice of a method teacher, who forced him into his method. After much instruction his swing "looked" better but didn't work as well. The new swing forced him to exceed his flexibility threshold, thereby upsetting his timing and swing sequence. As a result he wasn't competitive with his new swing.

A British Open champion and one of the top players in the world at the time felt he had to gain a few more yards off the tee, so he sought out a top teacher. The advice he got was good, it just didn't apply to him. This player is tall and thin, predominantly an arc player, but the advice he received was more suited to a leverage player. His swing no longer worked in harmony with his body, and he is now groping his way back to his natural form.

The moral of these sad stories is this: once you get "it," you'll keep it longer and get it back sooner if you have a gatekeeper. A major part of being as good as you can be at golf is knowing when you have it, knowing what you have, and then knowing how to get it back once it is gone.

On the other hand, it is possible to combine swing types if the match is correct. We have already talked about the great Greg Norman. His short-iron play was not as good in relation to the rest of his world-class game, especially with the wedge. Like most arc players who position the ball well forward and come at the ball from such a high position at the top of the swing, it was hard for him to keep the ball down. He'd hit towering wedge shots with an incredible amount of backspin, shots that were just too difficult to judge. He went to a knowledgeable teacher who left his one-piece arc takeaway intact but changed the rest of his swing to leverage. Moving the ball back and shallowing out the swing arc improved his short-iron play without sacrificing distance off the tee. In this case combining arc and leverage worked, resulting in successful hybrid—but please remember that this was a wonderful athlete under the watchful eye of a master teacher. As we saw above, it does not always go so smoothly.

It all boils down to this: be careful how you mix and match swing mechanics because what is magic for one swing type is tragic for another. Some mechanics fit together quite nicely to produce good golf shots and some do not. The trick in building and keeping a good swing is knowing which combinations fit with your body type. We've outlined a few of the basics below.

GRIP: STRONG VS. WEAK

A weak left-hand grip works for the arc player's hand- and arm-oriented release, but it's a mismatch for the leverage and width players' more body-oriented release. A stronger left hand (left hand more on top) is good for the width player because it matches the ball position, and it can also be a magic move for the leverage player with very quick hips. But without some major adjustments, too strong a left-hand grip is tragic for the arc player, whose club face would be too closed through impact. If you're hooking the ball with your arc swing, check your grip.

A weak right hand (right hand more on top) is correct for both the arc and the width player but not for the leverage player because it leaves the face open at impact. If you're a leverage player hitting weak cuts, start your adjustments by strengthening your right hand. Please note that too strong a right-hand grip (too much under the grip) is tragic for all swing types because it causes your club to swing too much around your body no matter how you're built. This error is a surefire way to hit wild hooks.

FOOT POSITION: AMOUNT OF FLARE

Something as simple as the positioning of your feet can affect the entire sequence of your swing; when this gets out of whack, you're in for a long day looking for your golf ball. For example, if you position your right foot perpendicular to the target line, you'd better be a flexible arc player. But this is not good positioning if you're a leverage or width player because a perpendicular right foot prevents you from making a level hip turn. If you tilt your hips in the leverage and width swings, you can't rotate correctly, and the position of your club head at impact will not be correct. As a leverage player, if you placed a carpenter's level on your hips while you swung, it would register with the bubble in the middle all the way through your swing. If you're hitting the ball all over the lot, you're probably got the wrong foot flare. Thus, flaring of the right foot is magic for width and leverage players but tragic for the arc player.

Your left-foot position can also be a swing maker or breaker. When it is flared out a lot, it encourages lateral motion, which is magic for the arc player, but it's tragic for leverage and width players because it delays the release of the club head to the ball.

CLOSED VS. OPEN

The wrong body alignment combined with the wrong stance width will earn you the nickname "wild thing" in a hurry! As you saw in chapter 2, a closed stance is correct for the width and arc swings (the heels are closed for the arc swing, but the toes are square) but not for the leverage swing. A closed stance allows a leverage player too much hip turn on the backswing, which causes the club head to arrive late for impact. In this case you either leave the ball dead right or flip your hands over and hook the ball. Neither is an acceptable option if you want to play your best.

If you're a muscular-advantage player, one of the worst mistakes you can make is to play from an open stance. Look at the closed stances of players like Duffy Waldorf, Peter Jacobson, and John Cook to see how it should be done. With your broad chest and limited flexibility, an open stance decreases your ability to turn behind the ball. It actually takes one of your greatest assets—your powerful chest—and makes it an obstacle to a decent backswing.

WIDE VS. NARROW

A standard-width stance is magic for a leverage player because it encourages rotary motion. A wide stance would be tragic for the leverage player because it promotes lateral hip motion that doesn't match this rotary swing. Conversely, arc players who adopt a very narrow stance lose their lateral hip motion; using only rotary-hip motion causes the arc player to come over the top with the right shoulder on the downswing. This is an especially dangerous mistake because they've set themselves up to pull the ball (straight left of target); contact is strong, and it feels great until you see your ball flying dead left into the bushes.

POSTURE: UPRIGHT VS. BENT

Posture dictates the plane of the swing; the more you bend from the hips, the more the club tends to swing up and away from your body. The more erect your posture, the more the club tends to swing around your body. Posture combined with chest size also determines the amount of arm swing; so a small-chested arc player needs an erect posture in order to create 45 degrees of arm swing. But an arc player has to be careful about standing too erect because the club will swing too much around on the backswing. The resulting error is an over-the-top downswing that causes fat shots and deep divots. You'll also lose power because you can't coil as well.

For the leverage player, erect posture is tragic because it limits arm swing, causing an early shoulder turn that reduces your ability to create a powerful coil in the backswing. It also encourages you to swing the club too far around the body, in turn causing you to lift the club to the top of the swing on a bad path. For the width swing, erect or even standard posture is disastrous because it causes the arms to lift away from the chest in the backswing. This forces an out-to-in swing on the downswing. That's when the big fellows' swings get choppy and weak.

BALL POSITION

Of the five areas involved in the setup, ball position is the most important because it affects each of the other four areas. A forward ball position is magic for an arc player; but if he moves it too far back in this stance, he gets to the ball too early and the ball will slice or be pushed to the right. Move it too far forward for the leverage player and the club face is closed at impact, resulting in a hook or pull to the left.

The lateral hip move and the dynamic leg action of the arc swing matches the forward ball position. This requires strong, supple legs and hips that allow you to spring at the ball without spinning your hips prematurely. Jack Nicklaus is a prime example of an arc ball position with very active legs. Nicklaus in his heyday was a hybrid arc/width player. He had the flexibility to swing the club in a long, flowing arc, and he possessed the leg and hip strength to play the ball well forward in his stance. His troubles started as he lost flexibility due to an injured back and hip and became a pure width (muscular-advantage) body type; the problem was he didn't change his swing to match the change in his flexibility.

Now, several times in each round, especially late in the round when he's tired and his hip is bothering him, his spring to the ball turns into a spin of his hips; because of the forward ball location, the ball starts left and never comes back. What was once a magic ball position for all his clubs (well forward off his left heel) now is a tragic position; lacking the dynamic leg action of his youth, he is not always sure where his ball is going.

If you're a wide body type with a big chest, you must play the ball farther back in your stance. If you try to swing around your chest to get to a forward-positioned ball, you'll have to push your club out and around, and that spells slice or pull.

TAKEAWAY

The arc swing works magically when you employ a one-piece take-away. But if the average leverage player tries a one-piece takeaway, the valuable left arm to chest connection is often lost, and the shoulders complete their turn too early, causing a weak lifting of the arms.

Starting with the arm swing first is magic for the leverage player, but for the arc player, endowed with great flexibility, using a leverage takeaway forces the arms to travel too far around behind the body instead of high above. For the width player, too much emphasis on arm swing causes the right arm to fold too early, trapping the club too far behind the body.

RIGHT-ARM POSITION

Folding the right arm early in the backswing is magic for the leverage player because it sets the club on the plane angle. It is a tragic position for the arc and width players because they lose their extension.

211

Folding the elbow early is magic for the leverage player but tragic for this arc player, who wants to drive his hands into the height dimension.

TOP OF THE SWING

There are three right-arm positions at the top of your swing.

1. Behind your shoulder with your right elbow pointing down to the ground as if you were throwing a ball
2. On the same line as your shoulder so that your right hand moves toward your head as your elbow folds
3. Your hand in front of your right shoulder with your right elbow pointing behind you, the so-called "flying elbow" position

None of these can be judged as either wrong or right, tragic or magic, until the body type is identified. For example, if you're a width (muscular-advantage) player, your flying elbow is a magic move. Because of your body type, the angle of your right forearm should match your spine angle at the top of your swing. The flying elbow keeps your hands centered in the middle of your chest, thereby preventing you from swinging too much around your body —the death knell for the wide-bodied width player. It also gives you some space between your body and arms so that you have room to tuck your elbow back to your side during the downswing. This tucking action is necessary to put your club on the proper approach path to the ball.

However, if you're a leverage player, the flying elbow can be a tragic move for you since your advantage is that your swing is always on the shaft-plane angle, a very accurate way to play. When the elbow flies, the shaft is forced off the shaft-plane angle, requiring some sort of compensation in time for impact to avoid pulling or pull-slicing the shot. Thus, for one the flying elbow is the centerpiece of the backswing, for another it's an out of control score-wrecker to be avoided like the plague.

DOWNSWING

As we have said elsewhere, one of the keys to understanding the LAWs model is the concept that some moves are simultaneous and some sequential. The leverage swing entails a simultaneous drop of the hands and shift of the weight into the left side, producing the signature bandy-legged position. This is a magic move, the only way the leverage player can take the most direct route to the ball. A tragic move is created when there is a time gap between the weight shift and the arm drop, causing the ball to go either right of target (shift then drop) or to the left (drop then shift). Ben Hogan's landmark book, *The Five Fundamentals,* was a fabulous instructional tool for many leverage players, but it killed off a lot of arc players who tried to start down by clearing their hips. In the arc swing, if this move is not preceded by the hip bump, the ball flies dead right!

The arc player starts the downswing with a pronounced lateral hip move toward the target, a magic move that gives the arms time to slot the club. The sequence can be described as shift-then-turn, and it is quite pronounced in the swings of modern players such as Paul

Stankowski and Fred Couples as well as the more classic, leggy-looking swings of Johnny Miller and the great Byron Nelson. The arms of prototypical arc players appear to stay above them forever, but this is because of the time gap between the weight shifting to the left side and the slotting of the club. Any other combination of shifting weight and turning the upper body and hips would be tragic because the time gap would be shortened.

As Scotty, the harried engineer, would always say to Captain Kirk when asked for an immediate burst of full power to propel the *Enterprise* away from some alien threat, "I need more time, Captain, I need more time." And that is exactly what the arc player needs during the downswing.

The width player has a turn-then-shift sequence where the upper body starts first, slotting the club in position; the weight shift follows just a millisecond behind, giving the characteristic over-the-top look of a Bruce Lietzke and Craig Stadler. Width players need the extra time before the weight shift is completed to get the club back on the correct swing plane, the one their club shaft had at address. Should the width player shift then turn (a tragic move), it would result in pushed shots that fly way to the right. Should they mistakenly use the simultaneous shift/turn, the ball is wild to the left.

Glossary

ACHIEVE AND THEN LEAVE Know what you want to accomplish during your practice session, and when you do, stop practicing.

AIM AND ALIGNMENT You aim the club face and align your body.

ANATOMICAL SNUFF BOX Term for the depression just above the joint of the thumb.

ANTAGONISTIC A two-muscle team giving full range of motion—e.g., biceps (flex) and triceps (extend).

ARC SWING Classic, high, arching swing, reverse C finish; no burst swing.

AXIS A straight line through a pivot point.

THE BALL AS MASTER The last ball flight conditions the next swing. Good ball flight, no adjustment; bad ball flight, adjustment. Not a good way to learn the LAWs model. The ball should not be your master when you are adjusting to the model.

THE BALL AS TEACHER Once you've learned your LAWs model swing, you make adjustments to it based on ball flight. The ball is your teacher when you're adjusting the model to yourself.

BLENDING Your arms do the up and down, your body does the around, and they don't get into each others' business.

BLOCKING Holding the right side leverage too long.

THE BUMP Lateral move of hips along heel line; part of the fall during arc downswing.

BURSTS Peaks of shaft bending during downswing.

CASTING Losing the left side leverage too early.

CLOSED Club face points to left of target; body line points to right of target.

COIL A ratio such as 2:1 where the shoulders turn more than the hips.

THE CONTINUUM A graphic representation of the relationships of pure prototypes and hybrids. The sides of the LAWs triangle that connect the prototypes. Sliding along the continuum creates hybrids.

CR's Abbreviation of collision requirements, the distances, speeds, and ratios of the hips, hands, shoulders, and club head necessary for efficient impact.

CUSTOMIZATION The final step in using the LAWs model is to adjust the model to you.

DELIVERY ZONE The part of the downswing where energy is emptied down the shaft and into the ball.

DIRECT ROUTE TO THE BALL Best, most efficient route your club head takes based on your body type.

DOMINANT DIMENSION One of three spatial dimensions, the one that all your swing mechanics are designed for.

DOMINANT POWER SOURCE The one source of power most characteristic of your body type.

DRIVE TO THE PERFECT The first step in matching up with the LAWs model is adopting all of the prototype swing mechanics.

THE FALL Beginning of arc downswing where weight moves from inside rim of right foot to ball of left foot.

FLARE TO SQUARE Arc players foot position in which the toes are parallel, the heels slightly closed.

FLAT/UPRIGHT An upright shaft is more toward the vertical. A flat shaft more to the horizontal.

FOOT FLARE Amount foot is turned out from perpendicular or ninety degrees.

FORTY-FIVE DEGREES OF ARM SWING Key angle in swing—aids in taking the most direct route to ball with power.

FOUR DIMENSIONS For LAWs model these are height (over you), width (away from you), depth (behind you), time (how long you spend in each dimension).

FRANKENSTEIN A mismatched golfer with swing parts that don't fit together.

THE GATEKEEPER The means by which you insulate your golf swing from the viruses that, once inside your model, will destroy it. This a major benefit of the LAWs model—it is a gatekeeper.

HAND SPEED Distance traveled in time; the farther the hands move from address, the slower they are. Also, hand speed in mph.

HIP SPEED As in how fast; can be expressed in mph or as a relationship, such as "faster than X but slower than Y."

HIPS/HANDS PACKAGE Relation of when the hips turn to how far the hands come from the top of the swing. Since they are a pair, strategies that slow the hips also speed the hands and vice versa.

HYBRIDS Swing types that have elements of other swing types blended in— e.g., a leverage player with a one-piece, arc takeaway.

INCUBATION PERIOD Time necessary to learn a new skill.

THE LATE HIT Hold the left side leverage until exactly the right time.

LAWs Acronym for leverage, arc, and width swings; the model for learning your swing, the blueprint of your golf swing.

LEFT-SIDE LEVERAGE Left side of triangle; angle between left arm and club shaft.

LEVER An arrangement of your body and club that multiplies your power. Left arm ninety degrees to shaft is one example.

LEVERAGE SWING Modern rotary, level hips, on plane; two-burst swing, low hands/high club head.

LIT Acronym for LAW's Identification Test.

LOAD Force on shaft, causing it to bow.

LOAD PROFILES (a) single burst; (b) double burst; (c) ramp up.

LOADING ZONE Backswing segment where wrists cock and coiling begins.

LONG SPINE Arc configuration where spine lines up with either hip. Long right spine at the top of the swing; long left spine through impact.

MAGIC VS. TRAGIC Swing mechanics that work for one swing type but not another.

MASTER MOVER The chest—when it moves in the arc swing, everything moves with it.

MATCHING TECHNIQUE TO PHYSIQUE Swing type is matched to what your body allows you to do.

MATCHING THEORY Sets of two parameters that fit together—e.g., long swing/slow swing; short swing/fast swing.

MOVING COIL Width players allows head to float back along with spine as coil take place.

OPEN Club face points to right of target; body line points left of target.

PASSIVE RELEASE The angle between the left arm and club shaft is lost, and energy is emptied into the ball when the hands run into the left wall.

PEELING OFF At the end of the takeaway, the three types move to their respective dimensions. The arc player sets the club up; the width player continues to push it away; and the leverage player sets the club head behind him.

PIVOT POINT A center of rotation.

POWER LEAKS Faults that cause inefficient energy transfer and/or delivery.

POWER V Right forearm bend into a V-shaped lever—sometimes ninety degrees, sometimes less.

PROTOTYPES Pure representations of each swing type—e.g., an arc player with all arc swing mechanics. Very rare—most are hybrids.

PUSH-SET Width wrist-cocking action where left hand pushes down while right hand pushes away.

RIGHT-SIDE LEVERAGE Right side of triangle. The angle between the right forearm and upper arm.

RUN OUT OF LEFT ARM Left arm at full extension during backswing—wrist cock happens at this point.

SEPARATION Hands move away from right shoulder during the downswing.

SETTING THE ANGLE Cocking the wrists, creating a lever.

SHAFT PLANE The lie angle of the shaft at address.

SLOTTING Proper move during the first part of the downswing when the club gets onto the correct approach path by dropping the triangle down.

SQUARE Club face pointing at target; body aligned parallel left of target.

SWING PLANE Should be termed swing-plane angle. The angle at which the club moves during your swing. Leverage players are on the plane angle; width and arc deplane and then replane near impact.

TAKEAWAY First part of the swing that ends in the peel.

THREE BODY TYPES Ectomorph—like a long tube; mesomorph—shaped like an upside-down triangle; endomorph—like a barrel.

THREE GRIP TYPES Strong—left hand on top of shaft with the shaft between the left thumb and the target; weak—left hand to left of shaft, thumb down the left side of the handle; neutral—left thumb on top of shaft with the back of the left hand to the target.

THREE TYPES OF ADVANTAGE OR POWER Mechanical advantage—power that comes through the use of levers; muscular advantage—muscle power; positional advantage—power from the height and length the club head travels.

THUMB LENGTH Long—full extension down the shaft; short—full retraction up the shaft; medium—in between.

TIME IQ How you will handle the time dimension.

THE TRIANGLE Line connecting elbows forms a triangle.

THE WALL Left-side barrier formed by lower leg, over which the club is released; a good release is passive.

WIDTH PLAYER TYPES Width 1—muscular advantage; (a) very large chest, (b) medium large chest. Width 2—players who must use the width dimension because they can't use the other two.

WIDTH SWING Hitters, short and fast swing; one-burst swing.

WINDOW OF VULNERABILITY Time frame when brain can be overloaded if given another task to learn.

Index